THE DELICATE ART OF

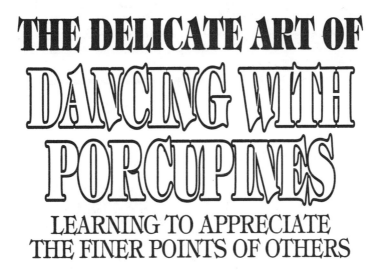

DANCING WITH PORCUPINES

LEARNING TO APPRECIATE THE FINER POINTS OF OTHERS

BOB PHILLIPS

Regal Books
A Division of GL Publications
Ventura, California, U.S.A.

The Delicate Art of Dancing with Porcupines is dedicated to the staff and board of directors of Hume Lake Christian Camps. I have appreciated the richness of their varied social styles and the honor and privilege of knowing them personally.

Published by Regal Books
A Division of Gospel Light
Ventura, California 93006
Printed in U.S.A.

Unless otherwise indicated, Scripture quotations in this publication are from the *NASB—New American Standard Bible.* © 1960, 1962, 1963, 1968, 1971, 1972, 1973, 1975, 1977 by The Lockman Foundation. Used by permission.

Other versions used are:

NIV—The Holy Bible, *New International Version,* Copyright © 1973, 1978, 1984 International Bible Society. Used by permission of Zondervan Bible Publishers.

Phillips—J.B. Phillips: The New Testament in Modern English, Revised Edition. © J.B. Phillips 1958, 1960, 1972. Used by permission of Macmillan Publishing Company.

TLB—The Living Bible, Copyright © 1971 by Tyndale House Publishers, Wheaton, Illinois. Used by permission.

Library of Congress Cataloging-in-Publication Data
Phillips, Bob, 1940-
    The delicate art of dancing with porcupines / Bob Phillips.
    p.   cm.
    Bibliography: p.
    ISBN 0-8307-1333-6
    1. Interpersonal relations. 2. Interpersonal conflict. 3. Human behavior.
I. Title.
HM132.P46   1989
302.3'4—dc19
                                                                89-31020

3   4   5   6   7   8   9   10   /   95   94   93   92

Rights for publishing this book in other languages are contracted by Gospel Literature International (GLINT). GLINT also provides technical help for the adaptation, translation, and publishing of Bible study resources and books in scores of languages worldwide. For further information, contact GLINT, Post Office Box 488, Rosemead, California, 91770, U.S.A., or the publisher.

Contents

Preface

Several years ago I attended a secular conference designed for leaders of various organizations. During the conference I was introduced to the theory of social styles as it related to people management. The content originated with David W. Merrill and Roger H. Reid, as expounded in their book, *Personal Styles and Effective Performance* (Chilton Book Co.). Although I had been exposed to similar kinds of material before, I was enthralled by the simplicity and practicality of Merrill and Reid's social styles theory. I returned home from the conference and studied the material further. I realized that Merrill and Reid's concepts constituted a vast reservoir of ideas for helping Christians get along with people.

I then shared the adapted social styles concepts with our staff of 70 at a retreat. I could not believe the response. The staff talked about the material for months. I began to share social style concepts at various couples retreats. Again I was overwhelmed by the excitement and interest displayed by the couples present. Since that time I have lost track of the number of presentations I have made and discussions I have led on the topic of social styles.

Interest in my social styles presentation was so great that I felt burdened to share these concepts with more people. So I considered writing on the subject. I was encouraged by the quote from Martin Luther: "If you want to change the world, pick up your pen." I wrote and rewrote the book repeatedly in my mind while I continued to speak on the topic of social styles on various occasions. At one meeting, I publicly mentioned that I was thinking of writing on the subject. At the end of my presentation a number of people said that they would anxiously look for my book. One publisher in attendance also encouraged me to go to print. During the next few days I considered carefully the comments I had heard. I decided that the embers had been glowing in my mind long enough. I fanned them to a flame and began to write. This book is the result.

I have not attempted to change Merrill and Reid's terminology in this book, nor do I deny the influence of the writings of Dr. O. Hallesby, Dr. Tim LaHaye, David Keirsey, Marilyn Bates and Isabel Briggs Myers upon my thinking. My goal for this book has been to adapt and utilize these excellent resources to present to the Christian community, as clearly as possible, concepts which will help us get along with people better.

I hope that you will find this material beneficial for getting along with the people in your life. It's my conviction that paying attention to social styles can help us learn even to "dance with porcupines." My prayer is that God will use this book to enlighten, strengthen, encourage and cause growth wherever it is read and discussed.

Bob Phillips
Fresno, California

Everybody Has People Problems

"I'm fed up. I'm angry at Sally and mad at myself. You would think that I'd learn . . . but not me. I keep opening myself up to more hurt." Laura continued to pour out her hurt and anger to her husband, Dick.

"I don't think Sally tried to hurt you deliberately," he responded sympathetically. "She just likes to talk a lot."

"That's for sure!" Laura retorted. "You tell Sally and you tell the world. Why can't she keep a confidence? I thought she was my best friend. That's the last time I'll tell her something personal. I'm lucky she didn't put an ad in the newspaper to broadcast my secrets."

Picky, Picky, Picky

"You can't do anything to please my boss," John complained. "I worked all week on the Carter project and he didn't even say thanks. All he did was point out four mis-spelled words in the report. He missed the whole thrust of the campaign just because there were four spelling errors. He even brought up the errors at the board meeting. I don't know if I can keep on working for such a narrow-minded, critical perfectionist."

Outside Looking In

"I'm worried about Billy," the young mother confessed. "He doesn't seem to get involved in the activities at school like the other children. He just sits on the sidelines and watches. Last week he came home with a bruise on his cheek. He got pushed around by some of his classmates. He won't say anything to them or fight back. He just takes abuse from other children. He is a good student and likes school, but he is kind of an outsider. I'm at my wits' end. I don't know how to help him."

"You Could Make a Fortune Renting Your Head Out as a Balloon"

"When are you going to start thinking? I swear, if brains were dynamite, you wouldn't have enough to blow your nose."

It wasn't the first time Janet had heard words like these from her father. She was criticized almost every time she asked him to help her with her school work. Dad didn't think she was very smart or that she could catch on as quickly as he wanted her to. He would sometimes rant and rave at her for over 20 minutes. She was torn between the need for help and the fear of the tirade that Dad would start. Janet wondered how much more verbal abuse she could take.

King for a Day

"I'm sick and tired of Frank's pushiness," Joe complained. "He orders everyone around. Who made him king anyway? He's no better than the rest of us. One of these days I'm going to let him have it."

"Remember what the Good Book says," Joe's wife responded. "'Do unto others as you want them to do unto you.'"

"That's easy for you to say," Joe snapped angrily. "You don't have to work with him."

If you are alive, you will experience conflicts with people. Your conflicts may be with family members, schoolmates, co-workers, friends or even strangers. It's not easy getting along with some people. But who said it would be? We were never promised smooth sailing when it comes to human relationships. Getting along with people takes effort. It means loving people when we don't feel like it and when they are not very lovable.

Helpful Tools

We all know that it is impossible to live without conflicts, but do our people problems always need to be so large? Is it possible to reduce tension in our relationships? Is it possible to keep conflicts at a minimum? Is it really possible to get along with people most of the time?

To be honest, there is no such thing as a perfect utopia for your relationships—at least not in this life. But I assure you that there are some tools available to help you get along with people better than you do. As you read through this book, you will discover some of these tools:

- a program for understanding your own social behavior and the social behavior of others;

- a means for understanding how you perceive others and how others perceive you;
- methods for creating and improving personal, family, work and community relationships;
- techniques for reducing tension and conflict between family members, friends and fellow workers;
- tips for improving your communication skills;
- ideas for increasing your tolerance for those who are different from you;
- and practical suggestions for demonstrating love toward everyone you meet on a daily basis.

No, you can't avoid conflicts with people. But, yes, you can work toward minimizing your people problems and maximizing the potential for your relationships. The tools are available. You can either pick them up and use them or ignore them. The choice is yours.

The Greatest Commandment

The basis for getting along with people is found in the words of Jesus Christ. One day a religious leader approached Jesus and asked Him to identify the greatest commandment in the Law. Jesus replied: "'Love the Lord your God with all your heart and with all your soul and with all your mind.' This is the first and greatest commandment. And the second is like it: 'Love your neighbor as yourself.' All the Law and the Prophets hang on these two commandments" (Matt. 22:37-40, *NIV*).

Jesus commanded that we must love our neighbors as ourselves. But who are my neighbors? My neighbor is anyone other than myself—family members, friends, fellow workers, even strangers. My neighbors are even my enemies, those who rub me the wrong way and make me feel uncomfortable. And Jesus directed that we love our neighbors with the same type of love we have for ourselves, with the same degree, and in the same proportion. To the extent that we guard our own feelings, we should care for the feelings of others. To the degree that we try to reach our own hopes and dreams, we should help others achieve their hopes, dreams and potential. That's not an easy assignment, especially since we often find it difficult to fulfill our own goals.

It's one thing to talk about loving my neighbor, but it's another thing to actually do it. When my neighbor is nice to me, it's easier to love him. But when he is impatient, angry, grumpy or aloof, loving him becomes difficult. And getting along with my neighbor is even more difficult in those times when I'm not getting along with myself. Have you ever been dismayed or disappointed with your own behavior? Have you ever asked yourself, "Why did I do that?" Have you put your foot in your mouth so often that you had to learn to whistle with your toes? Loving ourselves and our neighbors would be so much easier if we understood ourselves and our neighbors better.

The process of understanding our behavior and the behavior of others is difficult, and it is time- and energy-consuming. It's a struggle we will all face until we meet our Creator. But here's the good news: There are workable methods for understanding behavior and improving relationships; it is possible to begin to fulfill Christ's command and truly love our neighbors as ourselves.

First Things First

It is my conviction that getting along with people by loving our neighbors as ourselves is not really possible unless we fulfill the first part of the greatest commandment: love

God with our whole heart, soul and mind. Loving and getting along with people happens best in the context of loving and getting along with God. No matter how great a theory for interpersonal relationships may be, it will not work if we are not first committed to the practice of loving God. If you try to apply the concepts of social styles outlined in this book without loving God, your efforts will be manipulative and self-serving. Instead, we must apply these methods within the context of our love for God. Only He can give us the pure motivation and the strength to develop harmonious relationships. He will give you a heart of love for your neighbors even when they are most unlovable. He will teach you how to really get along with people.

CHAPTER ONE

Will the Real You Please Stand Up?

First thing Monday morning, Carl was called into the general manager's office. "Carl, I understand that there are some problems in your department," Mr. Martin began.

"What do you mean, sir?" Carl inquired.

"I hear from the other employees that you are hard to work for. They say that when you come around, you never say anything positive. You just seem to give orders in a matter-of-fact, noncaring way. They feel like you are treating them like machines instead of people."

Carl was shocked by Mr. Martin's comments. Carl had recently been appointed head of the production department, replacing Joe Swift. Joe was a disorganized, back-slapping kind of leader who spent most of his time—and his employees' time—just talking. Production was low under Joe's leadership, and Carl was determined to change

the department's image. He wanted the company to get a full day's work from every employee. Carl feared that if he got too close to his fellow workers he would end up like Joe. So he determined to maintain a businesslike posture. Carl wanted to do his best, and he wanted the manager to be proud of him. Now he was being called on the carpet for trying to do a good job. He was confused, disappointed and angry at the turn of events.

Misunderstanding the Real You

Like Carl, we have all been misunderstood by others. We have all said or done something, with pure motives and good intentions, which was misinterpreted. And we are hurt when others do not understand or accept our comments and actions as we intend them. Misunderstandings between people are one of the main reasons we have trouble getting along.

This common experience leads us to a question: Which is more important in social interaction and interpersonal relationships, the actual behavior or the motivation behind the behavior? Many would say that the motive and intent are more important because the motive causes the behavior. Others say that actions are more important, contending that no one sees another's motives, no one knows what the true intent is. We can only really see what others say and do.

I tend to agree with the latter position. This is not to say that motives for actions are not important. They are very important. The problem is that we can only guess at another person's motives. Sometimes we guess correctly, but most of the time we guess incorrectly.

Who then is the real you? Is the real you made up of

motives and intentions or of actions and behaviors? My guess is that, in the eyes of others, the real you is made up solely of what you say and do. No matter how important your motives are, people read you by what they see and hear, not by what you want them to see and hear. That's why this book focuses on our behavior—not our motives—and how it affects others.

The problem of interpersonal conflict is one of viewpoint. Our actions are very logical and rational to us, making perfect sense. Since we know the motivation for our behavior (sometimes), we falsely assume that others also understand the reasons behind our actions. We seem to forget that others are not always aware of our intentions, as plain as those intentions may seem to us. Others will often view our actions quite differently than we do because they cannot see our motives. In the minds of others, your behavior—positive or negative—equals the real you.

Behavior Speaks Louder than Words

Since we are going to focus on behavior, it might be helpful to explain the term. Behavior includes what we say, how we say it and all of our accompanying actions. Of these three elements of behavior, the most powerful communicator is nonverbal behavior—our actions. Next in line is tone of voice, and the least powerful element is our actual spoken message. Notice how the Total Behavior diagram illustrates the proportional breakdown (see illustration 1-C).

To illustrate the Total Behavior diagram, let's use the simple three-word message, "I love you." I will need you to help in this illustration by physically participating. If you are alone, pretend you are talking to someone you know.

Total Behavior[1]

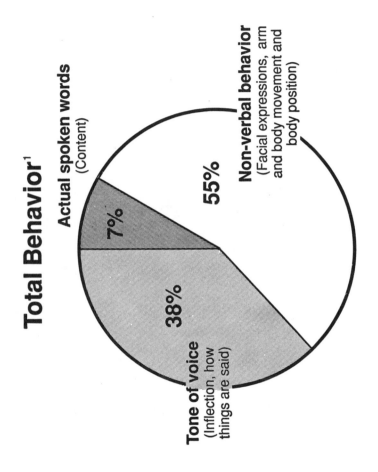

Actual spoken words
(Content)

7%

Tone of voice
(Inflection, how things are said)

38%

Non-verbal behavior
(Facial expressions, arm and body movement and body position)

55%

(1-C)

Clench your teeth and shake your fist at the person in a hostile manner and say aloud, "I love you." Do you think the person listening to your message will believe you? On the contrary, he or she will believe the tone of your voice and your nonverbal behavior, because they are more powerful communicators.

Let's try another experiment. Do not make a fist or clench your teeth. Instead, look at the imaginary person and say, "I love you," but put a question mark after the word you. Do you think he or she will believe your message now? Probably not. You have removed the nonverbal part of your message, but your actual words have been overpowered by your conflicting tone of voice.

Now try saying, "I love you" in several other ways. By changing the inflection in your voice or your accompanying actions, you can change your message entirely. For example, say, "I love you" with no gestures or emotion at all. The person listening will not be clear about the message. The words may be positive, but there are no positive tones or gestures.

Say, "I love you" and place the emphasis on the word I. Now you are saying, "If no one else loves you, I love you." Next, place the emphasis on the word love. Now you are saying, "I love you" as compared to "I like you." Finally, emphasize the word you. Now your message is, "Apart from others, you are the focus of my love." Three simple words, but how the message changes with inflection, tone and body language. [2]

If we want to learn to get along with people, we must become more aware of how people act than of what they say. Learning how others behave will help us identify clearly our own behavior. Hopefully, this knowledge will help us become more sensitive and caring toward others. Furthermore, becoming aware of how others perceive us will motivate our desire to change negative behaviors into positive behaviors. And changing behavior will help us build healthy relationships with our family members, friends and fellow workers.

A Matter of Perspective

The four professors had been lost for several hours and their safari in the jungle was turning into a nightmare. They had no idea where they were or how to return to their campsite. You might think that four learned men could solve such a problem. But these four men could not because they were blind.

The professors were holding hands and slowly walking along when they bumped into something. They couldn't see it, of course, but the four men had just found an old, docile elephant leisurely munching on some grass. The first professor reached out his hands and grabbed the elephant's tail. "It feels like some kind of brush," he announced.

The second man bumped his nose on the elephant's side. "It feels like a wall to me," he said.

The third professor wrapped his arms around the elephant's front leg. "No, I think you're both wrong," he argued. "It must be a tree trunk."

The last man groped in the air and his hands touched the elephant's trunk, which quickly encircled the professor's arm. "Egads!" he cried, "I've grabbed a snake!"

When trying to understand people, we always run the risk of misunderstanding them. This is because, like the four professors, we each have a limited personal vantage point. We assess people from our narrow perspectives and hastily slap labels on them based on personality, culture, religion, vocation or race. But like the blind professors, our labels only describe partial truths about people, representing our clouded viewpoints. Our misunderstanding of others is compounded when we mislabel them based on incomplete information.

Our descriptions of people basically fall into three areas. First, we describe people based on our view of their actual behavior. For example, we say: "He talks too loudly;" "Look how slowly she walks;" "His face looks sad and he speaks softly;" "She looks right at you and stands very rigidly;" or "He turned his back on me and would not speak."

Second, we describe people based on our thoughts about their inner qualities, traits, characteristics or motivations. We say: "He sure seems ambitious;" "She appears interested and sincere;" "I think he is a hypocrite;" or "She is very intelligent and honest."

Third, we describe people based on our emotional reaction to their behavior. We say things like: "He is definitely very strange;" "I don't like her;" "She really drives me crazy;" "I would like to get to know him better;" "She seems like a nice person;" "I hate him;" or "She seems trustworthy."[3]

Here's a practical illustration of how we tend to misunderstand and mislabel the actions of others:

Karen didn't take her usual morning coffee break because she was behind in entering customer orders into the computer. She didn't like having a cluttered desk, and she hoped that the extra 15 minutes would help her catch up. She was intently glued to the monitor to be sure that she would make no errors.

Sue, the office supervisor, noticed Karen working during the coffee break. She thought to herself, "It's great to

have an employee who is alert and motivated to the importance of filling orders so quickly."

Jane, one of the other computer operators, turned to
Betty and said, "Who does Karen think she is? She's trying to make us look bad for taking a coffee break. She's
just trying to impress Sue."

Bill, the sales representative, walked by Karen's desk
and said, "You're sure busy this morning."

Each co-worker had a different interpretation of
Karen's actions. Sue evaluated Karen's hard work positively, Jane expressed a negative reaction and Bill simply
observed her behavior without judgment.

Subjective and Objective Labels

Descriptions and labels that refer to a person's inner qualities, traits and characteristics are subjective. So also are
the descriptions of our reactions to the behavior of others.
Subjectivity is simply the formation of conclusions and
mental beliefs without verification. The descriptions by
Sue and Jane were subjective—based on what they
thought or felt Karen was doing—and they were wrong.

Objective description, on the other hand, is based on
real facts and observable actions. It is not based on emotion, surmise or personal prejudice. Bill's observation of
Karen's work was objective and correct—that she was
working hard. Objective description or labeling occurs
only when we talk about a person's actual behavior without
trying to apply a reason or motivation for the behavior.

In order to get along with people, we need to learn
how to observe actual behavior without attempting to
judge motives. When we react negatively to a person's
behavior or read into his or her motivations subjectively,

we tend to destroy the possibility of healthy and productive relationships. Sue's description of Karen, though complementary, was false. What Sue thought was dedicated service was only Karen's obsession with a neat desk. In her subjective description, Sue was setting up Karen—and herself—for potential future misunderstandings about her work habits.

Labeling others is not bad if our descriptions apply to actual behavior. These kinds of descriptions are not put-downs, merely clarifications of action. We need this kind of labeling. Without it, effective communication would cease. When I walk into the supermarket, I want labels on all the cans and boxes on the shelves. Without labels, grocery shopping—and the meals which followed—would be a disaster. Similarly, without effective, objective labels for behavior there would be interpersonal conflict and tension.

People-watching

Have you ever just sat and watched the behavior of people in a public place? It can be quite educational and sometimes very amusing. To help you learn to observe behavior more objectively, I suggest that, the next time you are in a public place (shopping mall, airport, doctor's office, etc.), you observe:

- how people walk . . . fast or slow;
- how people talk . . . loud or quiet;
- people's facial expressions . . . animated or controlled;
- the tone of voice . . . happy or sad, high pitched or low pitched;

- the individual's posture . . . rigid or relaxed;
- eye contact . . . direct or indirect;
- speech content . . . facts or feelings;
- body gestures . . . many or few;
- reaction to others . . . outgoing or restrained;
- response under stress . . . angry or fearful.[4]

We all tend to listen to others and watch their behavior half-heartedly. We then quickly move from casual observation to subjective evaluation and judgment. Many times our hasty judgments result in emotional turmoil and relationship conflicts.

A man and his four-year-old son boarded a train, and the man seated himself next to the window as the train pulled out of the station. As the man stared quietly out the window, his four-year-old became restless. The boy began to wander up and down the aisle. Soon he was climbing on the empty seats, yelling and singing loudly, and bothering the other passengers. All the while his father sat motionless, staring out the window.

Finally, an elderly woman sitting two rows from the father could not tolerate the annoyance any longer. She got up from her seat and approached the man. Her angry words stirred him from his deep thought.

"Sir, you should be ashamed of yourself," she began brusquely. "Your son is running loose on this train and bothering everyone. You should control him better."

"I'm sorry, I'll go get him," the man said. "I wasn't paying attention to him. I was thinking about my wife. She died yesterday and we are bringing her body home on the train."

No doubt the woman felt foolish and embarrassed when she learned that her hasty judgment of the man's motives were wrong. She exemplifies the words of Scripture: "What a shame—yes, how stupid!—to decide before knowing the facts!" (Prov. 18:13, *TLB*).

Here's another people-watching exercise for you: begin to watch the behavior of your own family members and friends. Do any of their behaviors seem to repeat themselves? Can you see any habit patterns in their lives? I'm sure you will. Learning these patterns or habits will help you predict how your loved ones will react in future situations so you can avoid interpersonal conflicts.

Take a Look at Yourself

Poet Robert Burns extolled the virtue of seeing ourselves as others see us. How do your loved ones see you? Can they predict your behavior? We like to think of our own behavior as less predictable than that of others. We often think of ourselves as more complex and more difficult to understand than others. Many times we look into the mirror and see only what we want to see. Francis Quarles wrote: "If thou seest anything in thyself which may make thee proud, look a little further and thou shall find enough to humble thee; if thou be wise, view the peacock's feathers with his feet. And weigh thy best parts with thy imperfections."

Take a moment to apply the observation skills discussed in this chapter to your own behaviors. Don't excuse yourself by claiming that your actions always depend on the situation you're in. You may say, "Sometimes I walk quickly, sometimes I walk slowly. Sometimes I'm angry, sometimes I'm fearful." True, we don't always behave the same way. But how do you usually behave? How do you most often react? Which behaviors are most comfortable to you? Which are least comfortable? Learn to identify your own actions just as you learn to identify the actions of others—objectively and nonjudgmentally.

The more we become aware of the behavior of others and ourselves, the more we will be able to control our responses. And learning to control our responses and reactions in our relationships will reduce tensions and help us get along better. It was wise King Solomon who said: "A gentle answer turns away wrath, but a harsh word stirs up anger" (Prov. 15:1, *NIV*). Our behavior and our reactions to the behavior of others can positively influence our relationships.

CHAPTER TWO

The Basics of Behavior

"I think we should strike!" big John Anderson bellowed. "Management doesn't care about us. All they do is polish the backsides of their pants in their fancy offices."

Ken Cryder agreed with John, but Ken thought that the workers should be very careful about how they presented their case. Everyone could be out of work for a long time if they came on too strong. Ken wanted to say something to John in order to quiet him down. But John was on a roll. In less than 15 minutes John had rallied most of the workers to his point of view.

Askers and Tellers

It doesn't take many years of living or a great deal of education for most of us to realize that everyone falls into one of two categories, illustrated by John and Ken. We are either more assertive or less assertive. We either take a more aggressive stance on issues or a less aggressive

Askers

- Less Assertive
- Less Aggressive
- More Introverted

Tellers

- More Assertive
- More Aggressive
- More Extroverted

(2-A)

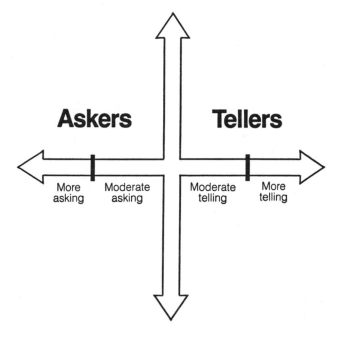

Askers   **Tellers**

More asking   Moderate asking   Moderate telling   More telling

(2-B)

stance. We are identified as either more extroverted or more introverted. For the sake of clarity and uniformity, we will call the more extroverted, aggressive and assertive individuals tellers. And those who are more introverted, less aggressive and less assertive we will call askers (see illustration 2-A). The terms askers and tellers are positive in nature and do not carry the negative connotations often associated with terms like introverted, aggressive or assertive.

While these traits are neither good nor bad, extremes in either case can be dangerous in relationships. If an asker never shares his feelings, he will be walked over by others. And tellers tend to overpower others. Each of us will display a different degree of asking or telling, hopefully in the moderate range (see illustration 2-B).

Are you more of an asker or a teller? Complete the exercise on the Clue Chart for Askers and Tellers (2-C) to help you determine which category of behavior better describes you. Notice that the column on the left lists 20 clue areas, and for each clue area are listed two ways of responding. For each clue area on the chart, check the response which better typifies you—asker or teller. Ask yourself, "What do I do more often? Which choice is more comfortable to me?" Then check the appropriate response. Total your asker and teller scores at the bottom of the chart to determine which behavior better describes you.

Task-oriented and Relationship-oriented

Gretchen bounced into the room with a smile on her face. Her bubbly personality seemed to lift everyone's spirits. She moved from person to person in the room saying hello and making everyone feel welcome. Her energy and vital-

CLUE CHART FOR ASKERS AND TELLERS[1]		
CLUE AREAS	ASKERS	TELLERS
General behavior style	☐ Less assertive, more introverted	☐ More assertive, more extroverted
Outward response priority under stress	☐ Flight	☐ Fight
Driving emotion and motivation under stress	☐ Fear	☐ Anger
Speech in general	☐ Silent, communicates hesitantly, lower quantity of talk	☐ Talkative, communicates readily, higher quantity of talk
Pace of speech and quality of speech	☐ Slower, fewer and more tentative statements	☐ Faster, greater and more emphatic statements
Volume of speech	☐ Softer and with little variation in vocal intonation	☐ Louder and emphasizes points through challenging intonation
Questions	☐ Tend to be for clarification, support, information	☐ Tend to be rhetorical to emphasize points, challenge information
General body movement and use of hands	☐ Slow and deliberate, soft handshake, relaxed or cupped	☐ Fast, rapid, firm handshake, pointing at others
Body posture	☐ Lean back while talking or making request or stating an opinion	☐ Lean forward while talking especially when making a request or giving an opinion
Eye contact	☐ Indirect, inconsistent, less intense	☐ Direct, consistent, more intense
Opinions	☐ More tentative and less forceful, reserves opinions	☐ More emphatic and forceful, shares opinions

continued

Confrontation	☐ Less confrontive, nonaggressive	☐ More confrontive, aggressive
Meeting others	☐ Tend to let others take the initiative, avoid imposing on others	☐ Tend to personally take the initiative, make presence known
Decisions	☐ Decide less quickly, will not pressure others for decisions	☐ Decide more quickly, will press others for decisions
Risk	☐ Do not like to take chances, like the old and familiar	☐ Like to take chances, like to try the new and different
First impression	☐ Likeable, shy	☐ Overwhelming, outspoken
Group response	☐ Go along attitude, supportive	☐ Take charge attitude, directive
Power	☐ Tend to avoid use of power if at all possible	☐ Tend to use both personal and positional power
When others talk	☐ Listen carefully	☐ Have difficulty listening
Response under pressure or stress	☐ More easy going, will withdraw or give in	☐ More impatient, will become dogmatic or attack
	_____Total Asking Behavior Clues	_____Total Telling Behavior Clues

My clue score totals indicate that I am a person who is more:

☐ Asking in my behaviors
☐ Telling in my behaviors

(2-C)

ity was contagious. Soon everyone was chatting happily.

Meanwhile, out on the patio, her husband Tim had just finished setting up some chairs for their guests. He returned to the barbecue to flip the steaks. All their friends knew that Tim cooked the best steaks in town. Ned, one of Tim's friends, asked if he could help. "Sure," Tim answered, and he put Ned to work turning the steaks. Tim went to the kitchen to get the cold soft drinks for dinner.

Gretchen and Tim exemplify two additional major categories of behavior with another dimension different from askers and tellers. Most people are either task-oriented like Tim or relationship-oriented like Gretchen. People who are task-oriented are ruled more by their thinking, and their emotions seem to be more under control. Their self-images are developed and they feel best when they are achieving a task.

People who are relationship-oriented, on the other hand, are ruled more by their feelings. Their emotions are more responsive. Their self-images are also developed and they feel best when they are accepted by others (see illustration 2-D).

In social situations, task-oriented individuals tend to prioritize tasks ahead of relationships. The details of the event are more important to them—food, decorations, accommodations, etc. Relationship-oriented people place relationships ahead of tasks. They are more interested in greeting the guests and helping them have a good time than in nonrelational tasks.

Neither trait is better than the other; they are merely descriptive of two generally different behaviors. Rather, either trait taken to the extreme can be unhealthy. If you are so involved with tasks that people can't get to know you or don't like you, you create tension, mistrust and

Task-Oriented

- Thinking Rules
- Emotions Controlled
- Self-Image Developed
- Individual Feels Best
  When Achieving

$$\longleftrightarrow$$

- Feelings Rule
- Emotions Responsive
- Self-Image Developed
- Individual Feels Best
  When Accepted

Relationship-Oriented

(2-D)

conflict. Others will see you as noncaring. And if you are so involved with people that you don't accomplish any tasks, you will be seen as shallow, not serious and maybe just plain lazy.

As with askers and tellers, task-oriented individuals and relationship-oriented individuals will also represent degrees of orientation (see illustration 2-E).

The exercise on the Clue Chart for Task-orientation and Relationship-orientation will help you determine if you are more task-oriented or relationship-oriented in your behavior. Complete the exercise as you did for askers and tellers. These exercises are geared to reveal traits of behavior, not personality traits or motivation for behavior. Personality is a much broader and more subjective topic. Our concern at this point is to discover objective behaviors and actions (see illustration 2-F).

Consider using these two clue chart exercises to help your family members or friends discover and better understand their behavior traits. Sometimes it is difficult for individuals to be objective about their personal behavior patterns. Ask your family members or friends to complete each clue chart as it applies to you, and offer to do the same for them. After all, in interpersonal communication, how you are perceived by others is more important than how you see yourself.

What's Your Style?

Combining your behavior style (asker or teller) with your behavior orientation (task or relationship) will reveal your personal social style. Askers who are more task-oriented we identify as Analyticals. Tellers who are more task-oriented we call Drivers. Askers who are more relationship-oriented are known as Amiables. And tellers

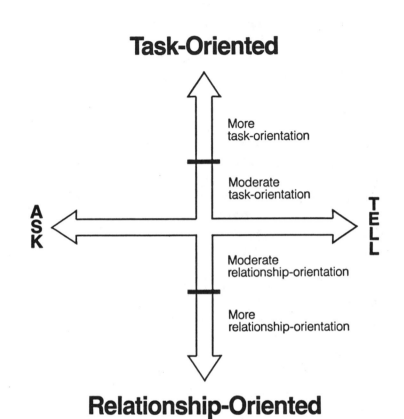

Task-Oriented

More
task-orientation

Moderate
task-orientation

A S K

T E L L

Moderate
relationship-orientation

More
relationship-orientation

Relationship-Oriented

(2-E)

CLUE CHART FOR TASK-ORIENTATION AND RELATIONSHIP-ORIENTATION[2]

CLUE AREAS	TASK-ORIENTED	RELATIONSHIP-ORIENTED
Priority choice	☐ More task-oriented than relationship-oriented	☐ More relationship-oriented than task-oriented
Dress	☐ More formal	☐ More casual
Tone of speech	☐ Some inflection	☐ Much inflection
Topics of speech	☐ Current issues and tasks at hand	☐ People, stories and anecdotes
Use of hands and arms	☐ Limited gestures and closed hands	☐ Frequent gestures and open hands
Body posture	☐ More rigid	☐ More relaxed
Facial expressions	☐ More controlled	☐ More animated
General attitude	☐ More toward the serious side	☐ More toward the playful side
When first meeting others	☐ Tend to be more reserved	☐ Tend to be more outgoing
Emotions	☐ Tend to hide them, to be controlled and guarded	☐ Tend to share them, to be more open and less guarded
General knowledge	☐ Filled with lots of facts and data, tend to make more specific statements	☐ Filled with lots of opinions and stories, tend to make more general statements
Small talk	☐ Tend to be less interested	☐ Tend to be more interested
Jokes and stories	☐ Tend to be less interested	☐ Tend to be more interested

continued

(2-F)

who are more relationship-oriented are called Expressives.

To help you identify your dominant social style, first decide if you are an asker or a teller based on the results of the first clue chart. If you are an asker, your social style will either be Analytical or Amiable. If you are a teller, your social style will be either Driver or Expressive. Next, based on the second clue chart, determine if you are more task-oriented or relationship-oriented. If you are task-oriented, your social style will either be Analytical or Driver. If you are relationship-oriented, your social style will either be Amiable or Expressive. One social style is no better than another. They are just different in their emphasis. Illustration 2-G will help you use the chart below to zero in on your specific primary social style—Analytical, Driver, Amiable or Expressive.

Ask your family members and friends to help you identify your social style based on their observation of your behavior. You may feel that asking other people to evaluate your social style is a little threatening, but do it anyway. You've probably wondered what they think about you. You now have an opportunity to find out. You probably already know your social style, so asking them for their perspective will simply help you clarify your understanding.

Now that the foundation for social styles has been laid, we will spend the rest of the book seeing how social styles apply in practical, everyday life. We will examine both the positive and negative sides of social styles. We will examine how each social style responds under stress and determine where the biggest conflicts between social styles lie. And we will discover how to get along with people—based on their different social styles.

Decision-making	☐ Based on facts more than feelings	☐ Based on feelings more than facts
Use of time	☐ More disciplined and less flexible	☐ More flexible and less disciplined
Supervision	☐ Appreciate supervision that gives goals and objectives	☐ Appreciate supervision that is concerned about me as a person
General attitude about rules	☐ Lean more toward the "letter of the law," more strict and disciplined	☐ Lean more toward the "spirit of the law," more permissive and fluid
Nonverbal behavior	☐ Tend to be slow in giving it	☐ Tend to be immediate in feedback
Sharing opinions	☐ More restrained, guarded, cautious and precise	☐ More impulsive, forceful and general
Relationship to others	☐ Tend to be a little hard to get to know, tend to keep distance	☐ Tend to be very easy to get to know, tend to seek the attention of others
	_____Total Task-Oriented Clues	_____Total Relationship-Oriented Clues

My clue score totals indicate that I am a person who is more:

☐ Task-oriented in my behaviors
☐ Relationship-oriented in my behaviors

(2-F)

TASK

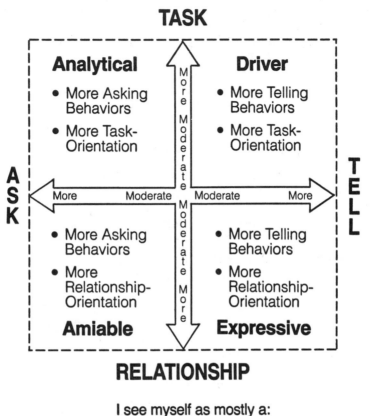

Analytical
- More Asking Behaviors
- More Task-Orientation

Driver
- More Telling Behaviors
- More Task-Orientation

ASK ← More   Moderate   Moderate   More → TELL

More Moderate Moderate More

- More Asking Behaviors
- More Relationship-Orientation

Amiable

- More Telling Behaviors
- More Relationship-Orientation

Expressive

RELATIONSHIP

I see myself as mostly a:
____ Analytical
____ Driver
____ Amiable
____ Expressive

(2-G)

CHAPTER THREE

Different Styles for Different People

"It's as plain as the nose on your face!" Martin exclaimed in frustration. "I don't understand why you can't see a simple answer like that. I can't figure you out!"

Why are some people so difficult to figure out? They think and respond in ways which are unfamiliar to us. And when we don't understand their responses, we often become impatient with them or distrustful of them. We would all agree that understanding the differences in people's behavior will pave the way for us to become more tolerant of each other and get along better.

One reason why people are so difficult to figure out is that each of us represents one of the four different social styles explained in chapter 2—analytical, driver, amiable or expressive. And each social style reflects a different combination of behavior (asker or teller) and orientation (task or relationship). We all tend to view life from the perspective of our personal social style and wonder why others don't see things as we do. This is where many of our differences, misunderstandings and disagreements arise.

Style Specialists

In order to better understand the four social styles, let's look at what each does best. Each social style is a specialist in one particular area of life.

Analyticals—*The Technique Specialists*: Analyticals have a strong sense of duty and obligation. They are driven by a forceful work ethic, and play comes harder for them. They are natural givers and often take on the role of parent or guardian for other people and organizations.

Analyticals often take on too much responsibility. They see themselves as conservators and tend to worry. They will save and store for the future, believing that they cannot save too much. They are steadfast, reliable and dependable. Listed below are some of the Analytical's greatest strengths:

The Analytical's emotions:
- Deep and thoughtful
- Serious and purposeful
- Genius-prone
- Talented and creative
- Artistic or musical
- Philosophical and poetic
- Appreciative of beauty
- Sensitive to others
- Self-sacrificing
- Conscientious
- Idealistic

The Analytical as a parent:
- Sets high standards
- Keeps home in good order
- Wants everything done right
- Picks up after children

- Sacrifices own will for others
- Schedule-oriented

- Detail-conscious

- Orderly and organized
- Economical
- Finds creative solutions
- Likes charts, graphs, figures and lists

- Encourages scholarship and talent
- Perfectionistic, high standards
- Persistent and thorough
- Neat and tidy
- Sees the problem
- Finishes what he starts

The Analytical as a friend:
- Makes friends cautiously
- Avoids seeking attention
- Will listen to complaints
- Deep concern for others
- Seeks ideal mate

- Content to stay in background
- Faithful and devoted

- Can solve others' problems
- Moved to tears with compassion

Drivers—*The Control Specialists*: Drivers are obsessed by a strong compulsion to perform. They take pleasure in almost any kind of work because it involves activity. Idleness will destroy Drivers. They desire to control and master everything they do. They speak with precision and little redundancy.

Drivers like new ideas, challenges and competition. They have a passion for knowledge. They are constantly searching to answer the "whys" of life. They can be overly forceful and may require too much from themselves and others. Many times Drivers are haunted by the possibility of failure. They are self-controlled, persistent and logical. Listed below are some of their greatest strengths:

The Driver's emotions:
- Born leader
- Compulsive need for change
- Strong-willed and decisive
- Not easily discouraged

- Exudes confidence
- Dynamic and active
- Must correct wrongs

- Unemotional

- Independent and self-sufficient
- Can run anything

The Driver as a parent:
- Exerts sound leadership
- Motivates family to action
- Organizes household
- Establishes goals

- Knows the right answers

The Driver at work:
- Goal-oriented
- Organizes well

- Moves quickly to action
- Insists on production
- Stimulates activity
- Sees the whole picture
- Seeks practical solutions

- Delegates work

- Makes plans
- Thrives on opposition

The Driver as a friend:
- Has little need for friends
- Will lead and organize
- Excels in emergencies
- Will work for group activity
- Is usually right

Amiables—*The Support Specialists*: Amiables are often found wrapped up in causes. They like to work with words and often influence large groups through writing. They work well with others and promote harmony. They sometimes place unrealistic expectations on themselves and others. They will often romanticize experiences and relationships.

Amiables like to have direction. They often observe others and seek deep meaning in relationships and experiences. They care more for interaction than action. They are very compassionate for those who may be hurting. They are patient, good listeners and filled with integrity. Here are some of their greatest strengths:

The Amiable's emotions:
- Low-key personality
- Easygoing and relaxed
- Calm, cool and collected
- Patient and well-balanced
- Consistent life
- Quiet but witty
- Sympathetic and kind
- Keeps emotions hidden
- Happily reconciled to life
- All-purpose person

The Amiable as a parent:
- Makes a good parent
- Takes time for children
- Is not in a hurry
- Can take the good with the bad
- Doesn't get upset easily

The Amiable at work:
- Competent and steady
- Peaceful and agreeable
- Has administrative ability
- Mediates problems

- Avoids conflicts
- Finds the easy way

- Good under pressure

The Amiable as a friend:
- Easy to get along with
- Inoffensive
- Dry sense of humor

- Has many friends

- Pleasant and enjoyable
- Good listener
- Enjoys watching people
- Has compassion and concern

Expressives—*The Social Specialists*: Expressives are very impulsive individuals. They like to try the new and different. They enjoy wandering. It is easy for them to break social ties. They like to live for the here and now. They struggle with commitment and follow-through.

Expressives have happy spirits and can endure hardships and trials easier than the other social styles. Discomfort is just a new experience which they know will pass. They like to reminisce and enjoy belonging to social organizations. They are friendly, giving and easygoing. Here are some of their strengths:

The Expressive's emotions:
- Appealing personality
- Life of the party
- Memory for color

- Emotional and demonstrative
- Cheerful and bubbly
- Good on stage

- Talkative, storyteller
- Good sense of humor
- Holds onto listeners physically
- Enthusiastic and expressive
- Curious
- Wide-eyed and innocent

- Lives in the present
- Sincere heart

- Changeable disposition
- Always a child

The Expressive as a parent:
- Makes home fun

- Turns disaster into humor

- Is liked by children's friends

- Is the circus master

The Expressive at work:
- Volunteers for jobs

- Looks great on the surface
- Has energy and enthusiasm
- Inspires others to join

- Thinks up new activities

- Creative and colorful

- Starts in flashy way

- Charms others to work

The Expressive as a friend:
- Makes friends easily
- Thrives on compliments
- Envied by others
- Apologizes quickly
- Likes spontaneous activities[1]

- Loves people
- Seems excited

- Doesn't hold grudges
- Prevents dull moments

In order to further understand the distinctives of each social style, consider the chart headed General Overview of the Four Social Styles. Note that for each of the specific areas listed on the left, each social style has a different and unique way of responding (see illustration 3-A).

Social Styles in Action

An excellent way to understand the behavior of the four

GENERAL OVERVIEW OF THE FOUR SOCIAL STYLES[2]				
AREA	ANALYTICALS	DRIVERS	AMIABLES	EXPRESSIVES
Reaction	Slow	Swift	Unhurried	Rapid
Orientation	Thinking and fact	Action and goal	Relationship and peace	Involvement and intuition
Likes	Organization	To be in charge	Close relationships	Much interaction
Dislikes	Involvement	Inaction	Conflict	To be alone
Maximum effort	To organize	To control	To relate	To involve
Minimum concern	For relationships	For caution in relationships	For affecting change	For routine
Behavior directed toward achievement	Works carefully and alone— primary effort	Works quickly and alone— primary effort	Works slowly and with others— secondary effort	Works quickly and with team— secondary effort
Behavior directed toward acceptance	Impress others with precision and knowledge— secondary	Impress others with individual effort— secondary	Gets along as integral member of group— primary	Gets along as exciting member of group— primary
Actions	Cautious	Decisive	Slow	Impulsive
Skills	Good problem-solving skills	Good administrative skills	Good counseling skills	Good persuasive skills
Decision-making	Avoids risks, based on facts	Takes risks, based on intuition	Avoids risks, based on opinion	Takes risks, based on hunches
Time frame	Historical	Present	Present	Future
Use of time	Slow, deliberate, disciplined	Swift, efficient, impatient	Slow, calm, undisciplined	Rapid, quick, undisciplined

(3-A)

social styles is to examine them in real-life situations. Notice in the paragraphs below how differently the four respective styles respond in the same setting:

Going Out to Dinner

When you want to take the Analytical out to dinner, you may find that he has a difficult time making up his mind about where to go. The conversation may go like this:

> "Would you like to go out to dinner?"
> "Yes."
> "Where would you like to go?"
> "Anywhere; it doesn't matter."
> "How about McDonald's?"
> "No, I don't think so."
> "How about Taco Bell?"
> "No."
> "Where would you like to go?"
> "Anywhere; I don't care."
> "How about Chinese food?"
> "I don't think so."
> "How about Italian?"
> "I'm not hungry for that."
> "What are you hungry for?"
> "Anything; it makes no difference."

When you finally get to the restaurant, the story is the same. The Analytical will scrutinize the menu like he has never been to the restaurant before, unable to make up his mind, even though he eats there often. The waitress will return to the table several times before a decision is made.

When Drivers eat out, they usually go to the same place every time. Why change when the food is good?

They won't even look at the menu because they already know what they are going to order before they get there. They will eat quickly and be ready to go before everyone else. There are better things to do than just sit at a table. For Drivers, eating is just another task. When it's over, it's time to get on to the next activity. As they leave the table, they will grumble about leaving a tip, if they leave one at all.

Expressives like to eat anywhere. It really doesn't matter to them. They will have a good time wherever they are. They like to try new restaurants and usually enjoy a wide variety of foods. They will try the strange and different. Why not? You only live once! It takes a long time for Expressives to place their orders. It's not because they can't make up their minds; it's because they are having such a good time talking. Expressives like to hurry through their meals if they are going to a party where there will be lots of people. Sometimes they will take a long time eating because of so much conversation at the table. They will talk to the waiters, the people at the next table and even the strangers they meet while walking through the lobby.

Amiables are easy to please when eating out. They will eat almost anything, not necessarily because they like everything, but because they don't want to hurt anyone's feelings by not eating. When asked what they would like to eat, they will respond, "What are you going to have? I'll have what everyone else is eating."

Amiables make good listeners for the Expressives at the table. They like to watch everyone else interact. They like to study the people at their table and other people around them. Amiables will probably be most concerned about leaving a tip for the waitress. They wouldn't want her to think that the people at their table didn't like her.

Let's Go Shopping

Each social style shops differently from the others. Analyticals like to compare prices. They will look at almost every item in the store, then go to other stores to compare prices. They will spend hours shopping for the best deal, even if it means driving all over town to save 20 cents. They usually end up. at the store where they started, because that's where the best deals usually are. They only go to other stores to make sure they haven't missed anything.

Drivers dislike shopping. They only do it with reluctance and a certain amount of resentment. When they enter a store, they do not like to be interrupted by the salespeople. They want to be left alone. Drivers are the fastest shoppers on earth. They will walk into the store quickly, look around hurriedly and walk out quickly if they do not see what they are looking for. They have been known to walk out of a store if pressured too much by a salesperson, even if the item they need is in that store.

Amiables have a little trouble with shopping. They like to shop, but they can be easily swayed by the opinions of the salespeople. Amiables might even buy something they don't really like because they hate to say no to a pushy clerk. Amiables really enjoy shopping with others, not for the shopping, but because they like being with others and having a good time.

Expressives like to shop and buy things on impulse. They like lots of color and especially enjoy sales. They are easily distracted and will sometimes forget what they came shopping for in the first place. They enjoy talking to the salespeople about anything, whether or not it has to do with the items being purchased. The salesperson may even be overheard saying to the Expressive, "Excuse me, but I must wait on some other customers." Expressives are hard to get away from even when they are doing the buying.

It's Party Time
At a social gathering like a party, the Analytical will usually spend his time with only one or two people. The Driver will move into a group and slowly overpower it. If the Amiable moves into a group, he will usually take part by actively listening. Sometimes Amiables will not even join groups, choosing instead to sit on the sidelines and watch people. They like to study human behavior. The Expressive will enter a party mouth first and will most likely talk to everyone at the party before he leaves. They are great storytellers and will hold everyone's attention.

A Time to Laugh
When it comes to humor, it's hard to tell what the Analytical will do. He may roll on the floor in hysterical laughter or respond by saying, "I don't get it." When Drivers hear or tell a joke, they will show little more than a slight smile. They rarely laugh heartily even though they think the joke is very funny. Amiables are the masters at telling jokes and not smiling at all. They especially enjoy puns, subtle putdowns and humor which has several levels to it. Their humor is very dry. Expressives like to laugh a lot. They can be seen laughing out loud, slapping their knees and poking and back-slapping others.

Give Them the Business
It is most interesting when the four social styles are in business together, because they approach life and work from different perspectives. Imagine that four individuals, representing the four social styles, own a business together. One night the factory catches on fire. Each indi-

vidual's approach to the fire reflects his basic attitude toward life.

The first person on the scene is the Amiable. He has just come from a fast food restaurant and drives up to the burning building with a Coke in his hand. He jumps out of his car, throws his Coke on the fire and says, "Someone's got to do something about this!" The second person to arrive is the Analytical. He jumps out of his car, quickly surveys the situation and says, "It's all over now. The records are burned and everything's gone. We're finished. We'll have to file bankruptcy." The next person to arrive is the Driver. He leaps out of his car, organizes a bucket brigade and rushes into the burning building to rescue anyone who may be trapped. The last individual to arrive at the fire is the Expressive. He gets out of his car, surveys the situation, smiles and says, "Where are the hot dogs?"

A Swing Set for the Kids

Imagine that each of the four social styles purchased a swing set, which requires assembly, for his children. The Analytical takes all the parts out of the box and lays them in neat order. Next he reads the directions very carefully and assembles the swing set precisely by the numbers. The Driver dumps all the parts in a pile on the ground, then begins assembling the swing intuitively. If he encounters a problem, he may look at the directions, but only as a last resort. The Amiable reads the instructions and then hires someone else to put the swing together for him. And the Expressive does not read the instructions at all. Rather, he goes next door to his Analytical neighbor and talks him into putting the swing together for him.

A Friend Indeed

In friendship, each social style has its positive and negative qualities. Analyticals are loyal friends, but sometimes withdrawn. Drivers are loyal, but often aloof. Amiables are warm, but many times conform. Expressives are warm, but sometimes fickle.

Styles of the Rich and Famous

In order to test your understanding of the social styles concepts and sharpen your skills of identification, complete the Social Styles Observation Quiz. The quiz lists 36 real or fictional characters. See if you can identify each person's social style based on your knowledge of the character. If you are in doubt, use the process of elimination. First decide if the person is an asker or a teller, which will narrow your choice to either Analytical and Amiable or Driver and Expressive. Then decide if the individual is task-oriented or relationship-oriented, leading you to one social style. Try to complete the entire quiz before you consult the answers at the bottom (see illustration 3-B).

SOCIAL STYLE OBSERVATION QUIZ[3]				
INDIVIDUAL	ANALYTICAL	DRIVER	AMIABLE	EXPRESSIVE
1. Hitler—political leader				
2. Bob Hope—entertainer				
3. Albert Einstein—scientist				
4. Bing Crosby—singer				
5. Paul the Apostle—Bible				
6. Johnny Carson—entertainer				
7. Sherlock Holmes—sleuth				
8. Dick Clark—TV personality				
9. Gerald Ford—former president				
10. Woodrow Wilson—former president				
11. Richard Nixon—former president				
12. Ronald Reagan—former president				
13. Peter the Apostle—Bible				
14. Bill Cosby—TV personality				
15. Jezebel—Bible				
16. Clint Eastwood—movie actor				
17. Thomas the Apostle—Bible				
18. Winston Churchill—leader				
19. Moses—Bible				
20. John Denver—singer				
21. Esau—Bible				
22. Jacob—Bible				
23. Lucy—Peanuts comic stirp				
24. Abraham—Bible				
25. Carol Burnett—entertainer				
26. Esther—Bible				
27. Dan Rather—newscaster				
28. Mother of James & John—Bible				
29. Agatha Christie—writer				
30. Dr. Luke—Bible				
31. William Buckley—writer				
32. Barnabas—Bible				
33. Commander Kirk—Star Trek				
34. Dr. McCoy—Star Trek				
35. Spock—Star Trek				
36. Scotty—Star Trek				

ANSWERS: 1. Driver; 2. Expressive; 3. Analytical; 4. Amiable; 5. Driver; 6. Expressive; 7. Analytical; 8. Amiable; 9. Amiable; 10. Analytical; 11. Driver; 12. Expressive; 13. Expressive; 14. Amiable; 15. Expressive; 16. Driver; 17. Analytical; 18. Expressive; 19. Analytical; 20. Amiable; 21. Expressive; 22. Driver; 23. Driver; 24. Amiable; 25. Expressive; 26. Amiable; 27. Driver; 28. Driver; 29. Analytical; 30. Analytical; 31. Analytical; 32. Amiable; 33. Expressive; 34. Driver; 35. Analytical; 36. Amiable.

CHAPTER FOUR

I've Got a Question!

Wherever I present the material about social styles, many questions arise. Most of them are for clarification and understanding. Some of them are posed in the form of a challenge. Interestingly, the types of questions asked and the ways in which they are asked often identify the social styles of the individuals asking the questions. Each social style approaches the material from its own unique vantage point.

In this chapter I want to present 12 of the questions I am most frequently asked about social styles, and my responses.

1. Are social styles like the signs of the zodiac?

No. Social styles do not depend on positions of the stars or dates of birth to determine or regulate how a person behaves or responds. Social styles theory simply seeks to identify habit patterns in individuals' behaviors. The four consistent behavior patterns which continually reappear have been categorized as Analytical, Driver, Amiable and Expressive.

2. Doesn't the social styles system put people in boxes and rob them of their uniqueness and individuality?
Not really. Social styles are something like fingerprints. Everyone has fingerprints, and each person's fingerprints are, at the same time, similar to others and distinctly unique. That's the way it is with behavior. Much of human behavior is similar, but, at the same time, each person has his own unique and individual "behavior-print." Social styles concepts don't put people in boxes; the system merely attempts to identify the behaviors a person already displays.

How a person responds in a given situation will be similar to how others would respond. The minor variations within a general response will be due to factors of age, education, environment, experience, understanding, social style, and spiritual relationship to God (or lack of it). Understanding social styles does not mean we can predict how each individual will respond in every given situation. It does, however, alert us to the probability of certain behaviors under certain conditions.

3. Can social styles be changed?
I personally think it is impossible to change your basic social style. I believe our social styles are intrinsic to our basic, God-given, individual make-up.

Nor is there any reason for you to change your style. There is no better or best style. Each social style has its own unique and positive contribution to make in interpersonal relationships. It would be terribly boring if all of us were the same style. God has made us different from each other—let's enjoy the difference.

The apostle Paul addresses this concept in Romans 12:4-6: "For just as we have many members in one body and all the members do not have the same function, so we, who are many, are one body in Christ, and individually members one of another. And since we have gifts that differ according to the grace given to us, let each exercise them accordingly." Social styles are like spiritual gifts: God has given them to us as He wills, and we must learn to use them appropriately.

Furthermore, your God-given social style has also been shaped by family and social influences as well as your personal experiences. The following equation illustrates the elements which combine to determine how you behave:

Your basic social style inherited at birth

+

family and society input and reinforcement

+

personal experience and developed habit patterns

=

your personal style of behavior.

To illustrate the influence of family on our social styles, complete the Short Family Tree chart. Fill in the names of grandparents and parents, and list your siblings from left to right in order of birth, including yourself (see illustration 4-A).

In the spaces below, list five descriptive personality or character traits for each individual. Descriptive words

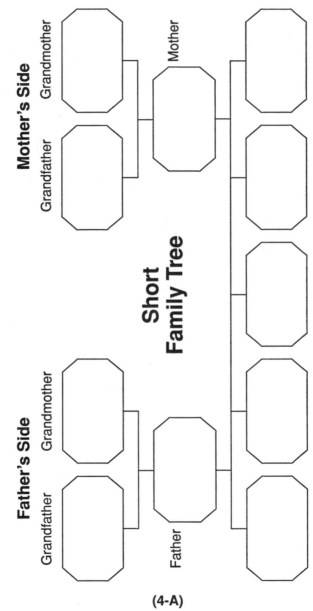

Short Family Tree

Father's Side

Grandmother

Grandfather

Father

Mother's Side

Grandmother

Grandfather

Mother

(4-A)

might include patient, harsh, kind, undisciplined, talkative, etc. If you do not (or did not) know some of the individuals, list traits you have heard others use in describing these relatives·

Father's Side	Mother's Side
Grandfather	Grandfather
1.	1.
2.	2.
3.	3.
4.	4.
5.	5.
Grandmother	Grandmother
1.	1.
2.	2.
3.	3.
4.	4.
5.	5.
Father	Mother
1.	1.
2.	2.
3.	3.
4.	4.
5.	5.

Are you more like your father or your mother (check one)? Father ___ Mother ___. Answer the next question based on the parent you are more like: are you more like your grandfather or grandmother on that side of the family (check one)? Grandfather ___ Grandmother ___.

Now look at the descriptive traits you have listed for the parent and grandparent you have chosen. Are the traits listed also descriptive of you? I'm sure you will find many similarities. You can repeat the process for each of your brothers and sisters and see how they exemplify the family pattern in some way.

We cannot separate ourselves from the influence of inherited traits or the positive and negative influences of our environment. This concept is reflected in the words of God to Moses in Exodus 34:6-7: "The Lord, the Lord God, compassionate and gracious, slow to anger, and abounding in lovingkindness and truth; who keeps loving kindness for thousands, who forgives iniquity, transgression and sin; yet He will by no means leave the guilty unpunished, visiting the iniquity of fathers on the children and on the grandchildren to the third and fourth generations."

The influence of family is graphically illustrated in the lives of two men: Jonathan Edwards and Max Jukes:

> Jonathan Edwards married a devout Christian girl and from their union came 729 descendants. From their family line came 300 ministers, 65 college professors, 13 university presidents, 60 authors, three U.S. congressmen, and one vice-president of the United States. They did have one noticeable black sheep who was Aaron Burr, a brilliant politician who turned away from the faith of the family.
>
> On the other hand, Max Jukes and his wife were unbelievers. From their marriage they produced 1,026 known descendants. Their children cost the state much money and did not give much to society. Of their family line, 300 died early in life, 100 went to prison for an average of 13 years each, 200 were public prostitutes, and 100 were drunkards.[1]

4. Are you sure we can't change our social styles? I find that I behave differently in different situations.
Yes, we do act differently at times depending on a number of factors. You have a "public you" and a "private you," suggesting that we sometimes behave differently when we're alone and when we're with people. When a situation requires it, we can respond more assertively or less assertively than we usually do. We can also change from being task-oriented to being relationship-oriented, or vice versa, under certain conditions. But the ability to change temporarily or situationally does not alter our basic style. It just means that we are able to flex and adapt when necessary.

A person can learn to smile on the outside when he is really angry inside. He can help others when he would rather work on his own project. Your job may require you to work with lots of people on a daily basis, and so you do, even though you may not be relationship-oriented. You may be very shy, but you have learned to respond differently in social situations where you cannot be shy. (Many entertainers adapt in this way.) Your work or community position may require you to speak publicly even though you are not a teller. There are many Analytical and Amiable ministers who speak to crowds several times a week.

We all have the ability to behave differently from our prominent social style when the situation requires it. But when the need for the behavior change is no longer apparent, we will usually drop back into the familiar and comfortable patterns of our basic social styles.

5. Are you saying that behavior cannot change?
Of course not. Individual behaviors can be changed or modified, but your basic behavior style (asker or teller), your behavior orientation (task or relationship) and your

social style (Analytical, Driver, Amiable or Expressive) will not.

Within each social style there are both positive and negative behaviors. Here are where the changes need to take place—accentuate the positives and eliminate the negatives. We will discuss the details of behavior changes within social styles in the chapters ahead.

6. Can the social style concept be misused?

Yes. It has been misused in the past and probably will be misused in the future. The social style concept has sometimes been misused in name-calling: "You're a Driver, you run over people;" "You're an Expressive, just one big mouth;" "You're an Analytical, you think you're always right;" or "You're an Amiable, you're just lazy." But people who name-call will do that with any system that's handy. People who put down others usually do so because they are miserable and they want others to join them. Sometimes they do it because they are guilty of the same behavior and deserve the same "name." Others belittle people because they want to elevate themselves.

Social styles are misused when they become an excuse for negative behavior. I may say, "I know I was a little harsh, but I'm a Driver," as if my social style gives me the right to hurt others.

Social styles are misused when someone endeavors to employ the information to manipulate others for selfish means. For example, a salesman may say, "If I tell lots of emotional stories to this Expressive customer, I will make a sale."

Social styles are also misused when they become a tool for determining or judging motives instead of behavior. For example: "She is such a perfectionist, she just wants to be judge and jury all wrapped into one;" or "He pre-

System Comparison[2]

SYSTEM	High Relationship, More Talk	High Task, More Talk	High Task, More Ask	High Relationship, More Ask
Four Temperament Theory—Hippocrates, O. Hallesby, LaHaye	Sanguine	Choleric	Melancholy	Phlegmatic
Jay Hall	Synergistic	Win-lose	Yield-lose	Lose-leave
William Marston	Inducement of others	Dominance	Steadiness	Compliance
Donald T. Simpson	Integration	Power	Suppression	Denial
Stuart Atkins	Adapting-dealing	Controlling-talking	Supporting-giving	Conserving-holding
Bill Sloan	Feelers	Sensors	Intuitors	Thinkers
Adickes	Dogmatic	Agnostic	Innovative	Traditional
Thomas-Kilmann	Collaborating	Competing	Accommodating	Avoiding
Robert E. Lefton	Dominant-warm	Dominant-hostile	Submissive-hostile	Submissive-warm
Theodore Levitt	Perceptive thinkers	Intuitive thinkers	Systematic thinkers	Receptive thinkers
Spranger	Artistic	Theoretic	Religious	Economic
Keirsey-Bates	Dionysian	Promethean	Epimethean	Apollonian
Myers-Briggs	Perceptive types	Intuitive types	Sensing types	Judging types
David Kolb	Accommodator	Converger	Assimilator	Diverger
Kahler	Rebel	Workaholic	Dreamer	Reactor
David W. Merrill Roger H. Reid	Expressive	Driver	Analytical	Amiable

(4-B)

tends to be a diplomat, but he's just an apple polisher." The social styles system helps us identify, classify and predict the future behavior of ourselves and others, but it is not to be a measuring stick for motives.

7. Isn't the social styles program similar to other programs? Without a doubt. The concept of social styles as outlined by David W. Merrill and Roger H. Reid is not new. The basic ideas have been around for centuries, dating back to Hippocrates (460-370 B.C.). The social styles theory has been called by different names, but the basic foundation is the same. Various individuals have used this concept of understanding behavior to design programs for improving sales, becoming more effective leaders and facilitating better communication.

The System Comparison chart reveals the variety of terms which have been used to describe the same four basic social styles. Most of the systems listed were designed for management training in the business sector (see illustration 4-B).

After hundreds of hours reading and reviewing these systems and countless speaking engagements on the topic, I have become most comfortable with the social styles concept developed by Merrill and Reid as presented in their book, *Personal Styles and Effective Performance* (Chilton Book Co.). They use terms which can be easily understood by the layman and applied to daily life. Dr. Tim LaHaye's book, *Your Temperament: Discover Its Potential* (Tyndale House Publishers), will give additional information regarding the development of the four styles of social behavior. If you want to do further study, consider the books listed in the bibliography.

The bottom line question for any system is, "Does it work? Does it help me understand my behavior and the behavior of others? Does it really help me get along with people?" For me, the social styles concept answers with a resounding yes.

8. *Can social styles be observed in children?*
Without question. It is fairly easy to identify children who are more assertive (tellers) and less assertive (askers), and those who are task-oriented and relationship-oriented. Even when they are babies we can see major differences in their behavior. Analytical and Amiable babies are often very easygoing, quiet and cuddly, whereas Driver and Expressive babies are often restless, loud and very active.

Many times cuddly babies receive more physical touching because they are easy to touch and respond well to being touched and held. On the other hand, active babies don't lend themselves to much holding. They push away and move around a lot. As they grow older, they climb off of laps quickly because they want to do something more active and playful.

The parents of a restless baby sometimes feel like the child does not love them. As the child pushes away, the parents feel somewhat rejected. What the parents do not realize is that Driver and Expressive children need to be active, not passive. They need to move and explore. The wise parents of active children will employ more active forms of physical affection, such as wrestling, tickling or tossing them in the air. Drivers and Expressives will not reject this kind of affection, they will thrive on it.

Active children may love activity so much that it is difficult for them to slow down. They need to learn to alter this behavior at times, because there are times when they need to be quiet and still. Similarly, quiet babies who love to be cuddled need to learn how to play and become more active.

9. Do children understand the social style concepts?
Yes, they do. In fact, children understand the actions and behaviors of others before they understand the meanings of words. They know which of their relatives are loud and talkative, and which are quiet. They sense those who are very friendly and those who are reserved and introverted.

As children begin school, they use different words to describe the social styles of their classmates. They might identify an Analytical child as a "bookworm," a Driver as a "bully," an Amiable as "teacher's pet" and an Expressive as a "joker." The terms may vary, but the behaviors do not. When social styles material is shared with children, they grasp the concepts quickly and learn the terms easily.

10. Do I have more than one social style?
The social styles theory suggests that we each have a primary social style and a strong secondary social style. Your secondary social style is what makes you unique and sets you apart from others in that style.

In order to identify your second social style, you must ask yourself almost the same questions you did when determining your primary social style. For example, let's say that you are primarily a Driver. Ask yourself, "As a Driver, am I more of an asker or a teller?" Having determined that, ask yourself, "As a Driver, am I more task-oriented or relationship-oriented?" If your answers to these questions are teller and relationship-oriented, then you are an Expressive Driver. If you answer asker and task-oriented, then you are an Analytical Driver.

The Primary and Secondary Styles chart displays 16 possible combinations of primary and secondary styles. In each combination, the secondary style is listed first, as an adjective, and the primary style is listed second, as a noun. Thus if your primary style is Analytical and your

Primary and Secondary Styles[3]

TASK

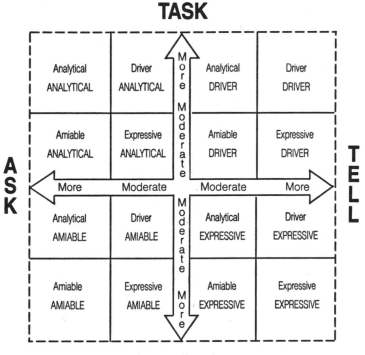

RELATIONSHIP

secondary style is Amiable, you are an Amiable Analytical, and so forth (see illustrations 4-C and 4-D).

If you have difficulty determining your primary and secondary social styles, and if you see yourself performing all the behaviors of Analyticals, Drivers, Amiables and Expressives, you are probably an Analytical. Analyticals have a tendency to see themselves in all four areas equally. When in doubt about your primary or secondary styles, ask your family members or closest friends. They will tell you.

11. Is the social styles theory Christian?

The best way to answer this question is by asking some other questions: Is money Christian? Is driving a car Christian? Is sex Christian? Is eating apple pie Christian? Money can be used for God or against God. I can drive with a Christlike attitude or I can drive like the devil. Sex can honor the Creator or dishonor Him. I can be a glutton at the table or eat in an intelligent, healthy way.

Like many things in life, the social styles concept is neutral. It is just a method of describing behavior which can be used in a Christian way or a non-Christian way. It is not a Christian concept per se. But it is a neutral tool which we Christians can employ in a positive, prayerful manner to better understand our behavior and the behavior of others. It's a means God has provided which can help us get along with people.

12. Does a person's social style change when he becomes a Christian?

There are three answers to this question: yes, no and sort of. First, yes, a person's social style will change in the areas of positive and negative traits. The indwelling Holy Spirit gives us power to increase the positive qualities we

I have been asked, "Is it possible to have some of the traits of all of the social styles in our lives?" The answer is, yes. But the percentages diminish rapidly after primary and secondary styles. Note the following illustration using Driver as the primary social style.

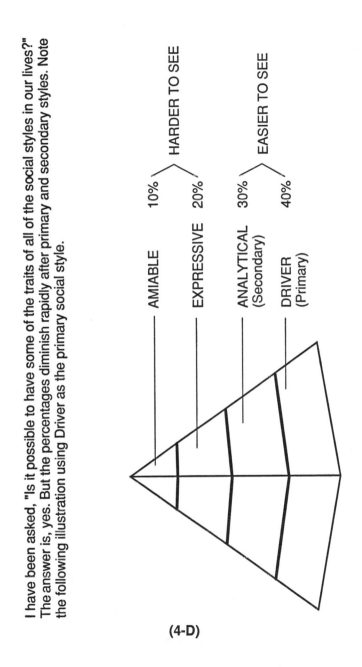

AMIABLE   10% ⎫
                    ⎬ HARDER TO SEE
EXPRESSIVE   20% ⎭

ANALYTICAL   30% ⎫
(Secondary)   ⎬ EASIER TO SEE
DRIVER   40% ⎭
(Primary)

(4-D)

inherit in our social styles. He will also help us change by
decreasing the negative weaknesses of our social styles.
Those are definite changes which God will affect from
inside the believer's life.

Second, no, our social styles do not change in regard
to our basic asker/teller or task-orientation/relationship-
orientation. These basic traits can be modified in that the
Holy Spirit will help me become:

- more assertive when I need to be more assertive;
- less assertive when I need to be less assertive;
- more people-centered when I need to be people-
  centered;
- more task-centered when I need to be task-
  centered.

These are not really changes in social style, they are
adjustments in response to the sensitivity to the needs of
others which God brings into our lives. For example, God
will help those who are more introverted to express themselves and take charge when they need to. God will also
help those who are normally more involved with tasks to
relate to people better. He will help those who relate easily to people to accomplish tasks they would normally find
difficult. And He will help those who are outspoken to
learn to listen. All these modifications are part of the spiritual growth process of becoming more flexible, adaptable
and versatile.

Third, sort of. These adaptations in social style to the
needs of people will not take place automatically in the new
Christian. They will only come about as he submits his will
to God's will on the battlefield of the two natures. Negative habit patterns are usually well established by the time
a person receives Christ. God can change these, but the

individual must allow Him to do so. He does not want to take away our individuality as expressed through our social style. Rather, He wants to cause it to flourish through godly behavior.

CHAPTER FIVE

Moments of Weakness and Conflict

George and Ralph played golf together often. One day during a match, George hit his ball into the rough and began to swear angrily. Ralph also hit his ball into the rough, but he didn't say a thing. On the next hole, George hit his ball into the water, and again he began to swear up a storm. Ralph also fell victim to the water hazard, but he kept silent. On the following hole, George hit his ball into the water again. This time he jumped up and down, and then he broke a golf club over his knee. Ralph's shot also plopped into the water, but again he showed no emotion.

Suddenly George turned to Ralph and said, "That's what I like about you, Ralph. You don't get angry like I do. Whenever you hit your ball into the rough or the water, you don't look upset at all."

Ralph looked at his friend and smiled. "You're right, George," he said. "I don't swear when my ball goes out of bounds. But wherever I spit the grass dies."

As George and Ralph illustrate, everybody has different weaknesses, and we all display our weaknesses in different ways. Many of our differences as individuals result from our inherited social styles. Listed below are some of the weaknesses found in each of the social styles. Compare these lists to the lists of social style strengths found in chapter 3:

Analytical Weaknesses

The Analytical's emotions:
- Remembers the negatives
- Enjoys being hurt
- Off in another world
- Selective hearing
- Too introspective
- Persecution complex
- Moody and depressed
- False humility
- Low self-image
- Self-centered
- Guilt feelings
- Tends to hypochondria

The Analytical as a parent:
- Puts goals beyond reach
- May be too meticulous
- Sulks over disagreements
- May discourage children
- Becomes a martyr
- Puts guilt on children

The Analytical at work:
- Not people-oriented
- Chooses difficult work
- Spends too much time planning
- Self-deprecating
- Standards often too high
- Depressed over imperfections
- Hesitant to start projects
- Prefers analysis to actual work
- Hard to please
- Deep need for approval

The Analytical as a friend:
- Lives through others
- Withdrawn and remote
- Holds back affection

- Suspicious of people
- Unforgiving
- Skeptical of compliments

- Socially insecure
- Critical of others
- Dislikes those in opposition
- Antagonistic and vengeful
- Full of contradictions

Driver Weaknesses

The Driver's emotions:
- Bossy
- Quick-tempered
- Too impetuous

- Won't give up when losing
- Inflexible
- Dislikes tears and emotions

- Impatient
- Can't relax
- Enjoys controversy and arguments
- Comes on too strong
- Not complimentary
- Is unsympathetic

The Driver as a parent:
- Tends to over-dominate
- Give answers too quickly

- Won't let children relax

- Too busy for family
- Impatient with poor performance
- May send them into depression

The Driver at work:
- Little tolerance for mistakes
- Doesn't analyze details
- May make rash decisions

- Demands loyalty in ranks

- Bored by trivia
- May be rude or tactless

- Manipulates people
- End justifies means
- Demanding of others
- Work may become god

The Driver as a friend:
- Tends to use people
- Decides for others
- Can do everything better
- Possessive of friends and mate
- Dominates others
- Knows everything
- Is too independent
- Can't say, "I'm sorry"

Amiable Weaknesses

The Amiable's emotions:
- Unenthusiastic
- Indecisive
- Quiet will of iron
- Too shy and reticent
- Self-righteous
- Fearful and worried
- Avoids responsibility
- Selfish
- Too compromising

The Amiable as a parent:
- Lax on discipline

- Takes life too easily
- Doesn't organize the home
- Will ignore family conflict

The Amiable at work:
- Not goal-oriented
- Hard to get moving
- Lazy and careless
- Would rather watch
- Lacks self-motivation
- Resents being pushed
- Discourages others

The Amiable as a friend:
- Dampens enthusiasm
- Is not exciting
- Stays uninvolved
- Indifferent to plans

- Judges others
- Resists change

- Sarcastic and teasing

Expressive Weaknesses

The Expressive's emotions:
- Compulsive talker

- Dwells on trivia
- Scares others off

- Restless energy
- Blusters and complains
- Loud voice and laugh

- Angers easily

- Never grows up

- Exaggerates and elaborates
- Can't remember names
- Too happy for some people
- Egotistical
- Naive and gullible
- Controlled by circumstances
- Seems phony to some people

The Expressive as a parent:
- Keeps home in a frenzy

- Disorganized

- Forgets children's appointments
- Doesn't listen to the whole story

The Expressive at work:
- Would rather talk
- Doesn't follow through
- Undisciplined
- Decides by feelings
- Wastes time talking

- Forgets obligations
- Confidence fades fast
- Priorities out of order
- Easily distracted

The Expressive as a friend:
- Hates to be alone

- Needs to be center-stage

- Wants to be popular
- Dominates conversations

- Answers for others
- Makes excuses

- Looks for credit
- Interrupts and doesn't listen

- Fickle and forgetful
- Repeats stories[1]

The Weaknesses and Strengths chart contrasts the major, more visible characteristics and traits—positive and negative—of each of the four social styles (see illustration 5-A).

When People Conflict

"You're not going out tonight!" Kerry announced to her teenaged daughter, Tina.

"Why not?" Tina demanded.

"Because," her mother answered.

"'Because' why?" the girl insisted.

"'Because' I said so, and that's enough! I don't want to hear any more on the subject. Go to your room!"

Life is full of conflicts, especially in interpersonal relationships when our weaknesses so easily float to the surface. We have all experienced and provoked hurt feelings, disagreements and frustrations in our dealings with others. In order to get along with people, we need to understand, not only our weaknesses, but our responses to the conflict situations our weaknesses trigger.

How do you respond in stressful situations when things are not working out the way you want? What is your first response when things are falling apart? When tension, stress or conflict arise in relationships, people usually respond in one of two general ways. We either tend to fight against or flee from that which makes us uncomforta-

Strengths and Weaknesses

ANALYTICALS

NEGATIVE	POSITIVE
Moody	Industrious
Critical	Gifted
Negative	Perfectionist
Rigid	Persistent
Indecisive	Conscientious
Legalistic	Loyal
Self-centered	Serious
Stuffy	Aesthetic
Touchy	Idealistic
Vengeful	Exacting
Picky	Sensitive
Persecution-	Self-sacrificing
prone	
Unsociable	Orderly
Moralistic	Self-disciplined
Theoretical	

DRIVERS

NEGATIVE	POSITIVE
Unsympathetic	Determined
Pushy	Independent
Insensitive	Productive
Inconsiderate	Strong-willed
Severe	Visionary
Hostile	Optimistic
Sarcastic	Active
Tough	Practical
Unforgiving	Courageous
Domineering	Decisive
Opinionated	Self-confident
Prejudiced	Efficient
Harsh	Leader
Proud	

NEGATIVE	POSITIVE
Unbothered	Calm
Conforming	Supportive
Blasé	Easygoing
Indolent	Likeable
Unsure	Respectful
Spectator	Diplomatic
Selfish	Efficient
Ingratiating	Willing
Stingy	Organized
Stubborn	Conservative
Dependent	Practical
Self-protective	Dependable
Indecisive	Reluctant leader
Awkward	Agreeable
Fearful	Dry humor

NEGATIVE	POSITIVE
Weak-willed	Outgoing
Manipulative	Ambitious
Restless	Charismatic
Disorganized	Warm
Unproductive	Stimulating
Excitable	Responsive
Undependable	Talkative
Undisciplined	Enthusiastic
Obnoxious	Carefree
Loud	Compassionate
Reactive	Dramatic
Exaggerates	Generous
Fearful	Friendly
Egotistical	

AMIABLES   EXPRESSIVES

(5-A)

ble. The motivation to fight is anger and the motivation for flight is fear. Analyticals and Amiables usually flee conflicts because they are the less assertive, less aggressive askers. Drivers and Expressives most often choose to stand their ground and fight because they are the more assertive, more aggressive tellers.

But a deeper, more basic characteristic underlies and motivates our fighting anger and flighty fear. This characteristic is the root cause of conflicts between people. It's the basic reason why people don't get along. It's selfishness. We clash with people because they don't see things the way we see them, or because they don't do things the way we do them. We subconsciously believe that everybody else should be like us. We are always right, they are always wrong. So I become fearful or angry when:

- I lose control of people and situations;
- I don't get my way;
- I can't do the job;
- I fail;
- I don't have good looks;
- I don't have money;
- I don't have education or social standing;
- I can't do what I want;
- I am not liked;
- I lose my freedom;
- I don't have answers.

So I flee or fight because:
- I want to eat the foods I like;
- I want to watch the TV programs I like;
- I want others to fit into my schedule;
- I don't like it when others cross me;
- I think I should be promoted;

Four Responses to Conflict

WITHDRAW

I usually tend to become less assertive, more controlled, hold in my feelings, keep quiet and not share my ideas. I basically avoid, dodge, escape and retreat from other people and/or undesirable situations.

DOMINATE

I usually tend to become over-assertive, autocratic, unbending and over-controlling, demanding that things be done my way. I have a very strong will and I attempt to impose my thoughts and feelings on others.

I usually tend to give in to others to keep the peace and reduce conflict. I appear to agree with others even though inside I disagree. I strongly desire to save the relationship even if it hurts me the most.

GIVE IN

I usually tend to emotionally attack others and their ideas, using condemnations and put-downs to discredit them. I have strong emotions and will tell people how I feel about things.

ATTACK

(5-B)

- I think others act dumb (but not me);
- I always want things to go right;
- I don't like rules;
- I want peace and quiet;
- I don't want to feel any negative emotions;
- I want to be left alone;
- I want to choose my own destiny.

Four Negative Responses

Within the context of our fight or flight approach to conflicts, there are four specific negative pathways that people travel when they face pressure. Although everybody has traveled each pathway at some time, usually one of the four is well worn in your experience.

The chart headed Four Responses to Conflict summarizes the major ways people respond to conflict. Which path do you usually follow in conflict? Which path would your loved ones say you travel? Place a 1 in the box which describes your usual first response, a 2 in the box which summarizes your second method of responding, and so on until you have ranked all responses 1-4 (see illustration 5-B).

Notice that the four boxes on the chart correspond to the four positions in the social styles system. This is because each social style has a typical, negative response in conflict which is the antithesis of its positive behavior pattern. If you are an Analytical or an Amiable, your number one response is more likely one of the boxes on the left—the "flight" side of the chart. If you are a Driver or an Expressive, you have probably found your first response on the right—the "fight" side of the chart. Furthermore, I would guess that you have entered your number 1 in the box which corresponds to your primary social style.

Back-against-the-wall Behavior

Each social style has a set of positive and negative behaviors. When the pressures of interpersonal conflicts come, we feel like our backs are against the wall. And when we are under pressure, we tend to shift from the positive side of our behavior pattern to the negative side. We become more extreme and rigid. We move into non-negotiable stances. Our interaction with others becomes counterproductive. Analyticals, who are characteristically precise and systematic, become inflexible and nit-picky, choosing to withdraw or evade problems. Determined and objective Drivers turn into domineering, unfeeling dictators. Amiables, who are usually supportive and easygoing, become permissive and conforming, giving in to others in conflict. And Expressives, who are generally enthusiastic and imaginative, become overbearing and unrealistic, resorting to explosive attacks on others.

As we focus on our own needs and seek relief from tension by expressing negative behaviors, tension rises in those around us. They then defensively switch to their back-against-the-wall behaviors. This domino effect of setting each other off leads to more disagreements, arguments, fights and wars.

If our first back-against-the-wall responses don't serve to reduce the tension in a conflict, we will usually resort to a second choice. Each social style has an ordered pattern for moving through a series of back-against-the-wall responses. For example, when a Driver experiences conflict, his first response is to try to dominate the situation or persons involved. If that doesn't work, he will likely with-

draw from the situation. If withdrawal doesn't solve the
conflict, he may attack those he blames for the problem.
And if he cannot win that confrontation, the Driver will
tend to give up and give in.

The chart headed Back-Against-the-Wall Responses
lists the common order of negative responses for each
social style. Although individuals may vary within a social
style, their back-against-the-wall behaviors will often follow the same pattern. (See illustration 5-C.)

The Nature of Our Behavior

The reason we wrestle with selfishness, weakness and
conflict in our relationships is because we all inherited
something more than our social styles. Thanks to our
great-grandfather Adam, we have also inherited a sin
nature. Consequently, it is the nature of man to be sinful
and selfish just as surely as it is the nature of a pig to wallow in the mud. People don't need to learn to sin any more
than pigs need to learn to wallow; we do it naturally.

The social styles of behavior we are discussing have
both positive and negative traits. Our sin nature pushes
hard on us to exercise the negative traits of our behavior.
Even when we are exercising positive traits, the sin
nature is there encouraging us to use those traits for selfish reasons. In one ear we hear Jesus commanding us to
love our neighbors as ourselves. But in the other ear the
sin nature clamors, "Look out for number one!" It's clear
that the old nature is not going to help us obey Christ's
command. We need a new nature, one that is equipped
with the ability to get along with people, one that strength-
ens our strengths and weakens our weaknesses, one that
is motivated by God Himself.

This new nature only comes when you begin to love

Back-Against-the-Wall Responses[2]

TASK

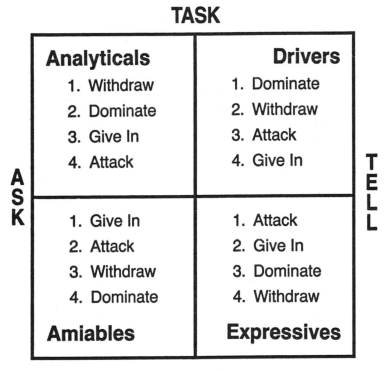

A S K

Analyticals
1. Withdraw
2. Dominate
3. Give In
4. Attack

Drivers
1. Dominate
2. Withdraw
3. Attack
4. Give In

T E L L

1. Give In
2. Attack
3. Withdraw
4. Dominate

Amiables

1. Attack
2. Give In
3. Dominate
4. Withdraw

Expressives

RELATIONSHIP

(5-C)

God with all your heart, soul and mind. How can you love God this way? How can you find peace with God and with your fellow man? It starts by personally inviting Jesus Christ to come into your heart and life. Have you received Christ into your life? Do you know your sins are forgiven and that God has placed His new nature within you? If not, how about making that decision right now?

When we receive Christ into our lives, we receive a new nature. This new nature empowers the positive traits and behaviors of my social style. My motivation is no longer controlled by the old nature, resulting in ungodly behavior, but I am motivated by genuine love, resulting in godly behavior. The old nature doesn't give up easily. Our lives become a battleground between the old nature and the new nature, negative behaviors and positive behaviors, weaknesses and strengths. This battle is described by Paul in Galatians 5:16-26:

> Live your whole life in the Spirit and you will not satisfy the desires of your lower nature. For the whole energy of the lower nature is set against the Spirit, while the whole power of the Spirit is contrary to the lower nature. Here is the conflict, and that is why you are not able to do what you want to do. But if you follow the leading of the Spirit, you stand clear of the Law.
>
> The activities of the lower nature are obvious. Here is a list: sexual immorality, impurity of mind, sensuality, worship of false gods, witchcraft, hatred, strife, jealousy, bad temper, rivalry, factions, party-spirit, envy, drunkenness, orgies and things like that. I solemnly assure you, as I did before, that those who indulge in such things will never inherit God's

kingdom. The Spirit, however, produces in human life fruits such as these: love, joy, peace, patience, kindness, generosity, fidelity, tolerance and self-control—and no law exists against any of them.

Those who belong to Christ Jesus have crucified their lower nature with all that it loved and lusted for. If our lives are centered in the Spirit, let us be guided by the Spirit. Let us not be ambitious for our own reputations, for that only means making each other jealous (*Phillips*).

The old sin nature, inherited from Adam, and the new nature from God are in conflict with each other. Both try to impact my behavior. Both try to influence my will. My will is the key. I must decide whether to listen to the promptings of the old sin nature or the influence of the Holy Spirit through my new nature.

We need God's help to win the battle. God will give us the wisdom and strength to curb our weaknesses, negative traits and back-against-the-wall behaviors. He will help us respond properly to others' weaknesses, negative strengths and back-against-the-wall behaviors. He will help us get along with people.

CHAPTER SIX

Helping People in Distress

"You just sit there like a bump on a log. Why don't you tell me what's going on?" Randy probed harshly. But Evie sat motionless, seeming almost catatonic. "I really get tired of your silence and pouting. You never want to face anything unpleasant. You go into your little world and hide. Hello, are you there? Is anyone home? That's right, go ahead and sulk! You want me to get your mommy for you? No wonder no one wants to be around you."

"That's the stupidest thing I've ever heard," Trish retorted angrily to Connie, grabbing her arm firmly and brusquely pushing her into a chair. "How could any rational person believe a word you are saying? You should lower your voice and speak like a normal human being. All you do is rant and rave and jump around like a crazy person. You throw your little temper tantrums and expect the world to bow down to you. Why don't you grow up and act your age? If you don't learn to control yourself, the little

men in the white coats are going to come and take you
away."

How do you think Evie will respond to Randy's challenge to open up and share her feelings? Do you think she
feels encouraged to share her deepest feelings and
thoughts? Of course not. Evie feels attacked, not encouraged. And as the tension level rises during Randy's confrontation, Evie has only one desire—withdrawal from the
situation.

In the second scene, Connie's "blow up" made Trish
feel attacked, and Trish responded in kind. Do you think
Trish's response to Connie's blow up will quiet the argu-
ment or intensify it? It's obvious that the situation is not
going to get better in the prevailing atmosphere of hostil-
ity. Instead, it may turn into a war. Both felt attacked and
responded with counterattacks, and soon they will be trying to out-yell each other.

When the Pressure Is On

Individuals express back-against-the-wall behavior for one
reason: to reduce the tension and stress of a negative situation or confrontation. Not all stress in life is bad. Hans
Selye, one of the foremost authorities on stress, suggests
in his book, *Stress Without Distress*, that some stress is
healthy. He calls healthy stress *eustress*, a positive, moti-
vating tension which helps us accomplish our tasks in life.
But when rising tension begins to threaten us personally,
positive eustress gives way to negative distress. Distress
destroys self-confidence, personal health, family unity and
relationships in general (see illustration 6-A).

When distress provokes a family member, friend or fellow worker to express his back-against-the-wall behavior,

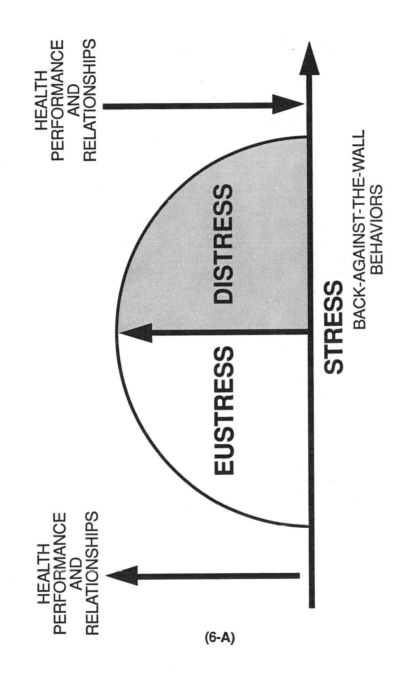

(6-A)

how should you respond? The nature of your response can either increase or decrease the tension. Consider the Bible's advice:

- "When there are many words, transgression is unavoidable, but he who restrains his lips is wise" (Prov. 10:19);
- "Don't talk so much. You keep putting your foot in your mouth. Be sensible and turn off the flow!" (Prov. 10:19, *TLB*);
- "He who restrains his words has knowledge, and he who has a cool spirit is a man of understanding" (Prov. 17:27);
- "A brother offended is harder to be won than a strong city, and contentions are like the bars of a castle" (Prov. 18:19);
- "A man's discretion makes him slow to anger, and it is his glory to overlook a transgression" (Prov. 19:11).

If we want to get along with people by loving them as Jesus commanded, then we need to love them even when they are not very lovable. We must learn to meet people's needs even when they display negative, back-against-the-wall behavior.

Each social style responds to distress in a unique way. Analyticals and Amiables take flight in fear. Analyticals withdraw from conflict to give themselves time to think. Amiables withdraw endeavoring to save the relationship. Drivers and Expressives don't take flight; they respond in anger and fight. Drivers dig in their heels and try to dominate the situation. Expressives explode and attack the conflicting situation or person. Each of these back-against-the-wall behaviors is a reaction aimed at reducing personal distress. Sometimes these reactions work, but many times these behaviors only increase the tension in others.

Here are some suggestions to help you respond positively to others who are expressing negative back-against-the-wall behaviors:

1. Be alert to how you are feeling. Do you feel your tension-level rising? Take control of your feelings. Don't let their behavior control you or determine your behavior. Don't let their behavior trigger your back-against-the-wall behavior. You can choose to allow God to control your feelings. When you sense your tension-level rising, pray. Ask God to give you a godly response.

2. Be alert to the subtle behaviors of Analyticals and Amiables. By nature, Drivers and Expressives are more open and vocal in their back-against-the-wall behaviors. But sometimes we barely notice the behaviors of Analyticals and Amiables because they tend to be quiet and reserved, even when they are reacting to stress. When you feel uncomfortable with their silence, they are probably acting out their back-against-the-wall behavior of withdrawal or acquiescence.

3. Be alert to the possibility that their behavior may not be directed at you personally. Sometimes whatever you said or did which provoked negative behavior in a loved one was simply "the last straw" for them. Other pressures may have been mounting up, and you just happened to be the one to feel the brunt of their back-against-the-wall reaction. Instead of responding defensively by saying, "You sure are a grouch today," you might say, "It sounds like you're having a difficult day. Can I be of help?"

4. Be alert to your verbal responses to negative behavior.

According to the Proverbs, your words can either curtail or perpetuate the problem:

- "Death and life are in the power of the tongue, and those who love it will eat its fruit" (Prov. 18:21);
- "Like apples of gold in settings of silver is a word spoken in right circumstances" (Prov. 25:11);
- "Do you see a man who is hasty in his words? There is more hope for a fool than for him" (Prov. 29:20);
- "A soothing tongue is a tree of life, but perversion in it crushes the spirit" (Prov. 15:4);
- "Pleasant words are a honeycomb, sweet to the soul and healing to the bones" (Prov. 16:24).

5. *Be ready to gently confront back-against-the-wall behavior.* Again, the Proverbs are rich with insight:

- "A man has joy in an apt answer, and how delightful is a timely word!" (Prov. 15:23);
- "A rebuke goes deeper into one who has understanding than a hundred blows into a fool" (Prov. 17:10);
- "Oil and perfume make the heart glad, so a man's counsel is sweet to his friend" (Prov. 27:9).

Responding to the Withdrawing Analytical

Analyticals tend to withdraw from conflict to save face. They want to deal with the problem alone, with a minimum of interaction with others. They need time to think about the problem situation or relationship. They need as much information as possible in order to deal effectively with their distress.

Don't keep pushing Analyticals for a response or insist

on their increased participation before they have time to think. Since Analyticals are by nature systematic, make sure you approach their problem with a step-by-step solution. Help them set up a plan to gather more problem-solving data to consider. Ask them for time to discuss the matter after they have had time to think about it. Slow down and be patient. Love them by cooperating with their method for dealing with problems and conflicts. They need time and space; give it to them.

Responding to the Dominating Driver

Drivers feel like they have lost control in conflict situations, leaving them with no personal choices. The tension they feel drives them to get something accomplished, and they may attempt to regain control by over-controlling.

Don't try to compete with Drivers or match force with force, because competition is their specialty. Don't argue or debate with them. They can verbally cut you to pieces in a hurry. But don't back down from them either, even when they come on strong. Drivers respect people who hold their ground, even if those people don't agree with the driver's position.

Try to redirect their strong energies toward positive goals, achievements or actions which you can support. Drivers appreciate goals and the freedom to choose their own methods of reaching their goals. Help them decide on a goal and a path for reaching the goal. Don't give in. Speak the truth in love and firmness. They will respond.

Responding to the Acquiescing Amiable

Amiables always appear to be in agreement during conflict. They will try to maintain relationships at all costs, even the cost of personal hurt. But don't be fooled. Their compliance is not a sign of commitment.

Don't try to press Amiables for responses. Don't express anger to them, argue with them or insist on your way. These responses will only push them deeper into their pattern of acquiescence as they struggle to save the relationship. Rather, encourage them to share their feelings. Ask them for constructive criticism regarding the conflict. Tell them that you would like to work on the situation, but that you need some concrete suggestions from them to help you. Amiables like to feel needed and to help. Work side-by-side with them through the problem-solving steps they suggest. Establish some kind of evaluation process. They will respond cautiously, so move slowly and be patient. Help them solve their conflict while they maintain their cherished relationships.

Responding to the Attacking Expressive

Expressives become very selfish, emotional and assertive when their backs are up against the wall. They will vent their feelings by attacking the situation and the people involved. They will not hesitate to chew you out and tell you what they don't like, and they will do so with gusto.

Don't try to evaluate an Expressive's emotional outburst or defend yourself intellectually. Neither will help, because his behavior is emotionally based. Don't let Expressives draw you into their tantrums. Don't shout back, because they likely have stronger lungs and they will shout you down. Instead, try to listen sympathetically and accept their emotions without getting emotionally involved yourself. Let them get their emotions out of their systems. If you block their venting, you may provoke an even greater explosion. Once they get their emotions off their chests, help them focus on creative alternatives for handling their problems in the future. Say something like, "Now that you have shared your feelings, how are we going to handle this problem the next time?"

Dealing with others when their backs are against the wall, and controlling our responses in the process, is no easy task. We need God's strength on a daily basis to put these strategies into action. Caring for others in this way is a true test of love. For the kind of love that can outlast back-against-the-wall behavior, we must return the pattern God has provided in His Word:

> If I speak with the tongues of men and angels, but do not have love, I have become a noisy gong or a clanging cymbal. And if I have the gift of prophecy, and know all mysteries and all knowledge; and if I have all faith, so as to remove mountains, but do not have love, I am nothing. And if I give all my possessions to feed the poor, and if I deliver my body to be burned, but do not have love, it profits me nothing.
>
> Love is patient, love is kind, and is not jealous; love does not brag and is not arrogant, does not act unbecomingly; it does not seek its own, is not provoked, does not take into account a wrong suffered, does not rejoice in unrighteousness, but rejoices with the truth; bears all things, believes all things, hopes all things, endures all things.
>
> Love never fails. . . . But now abide faith, hope, love, these three; but the greatest of these is love (1 Cor. 13:1-8,13).

CHAPTER SEVEN

The Friction Factor

"Can't you hurry it up a little, Susan?" Mark urged. "You're such a slowpoke. You know the old saying: 'He who hesitates is lost.'"

"Well, Mark, you're really the one with the problem," Susan replied. "You make rash decisions and always get yourself into a mess. Maybe you should remember the proverb: 'Haste makes waste.'"

"You may get a lot of things done in life, Dan, but I doubt if you will ever have many friends," Jack chided. "You can't always have your nose to the grindstone. You're already a workaholic—early to work and late coming home. You're going to have a heart attack by the time you're 40. Why don't you stop and smell the roses?"

"Yes, I work hard and long, Jack," Dan answered, "but, as they say, 'a rolling stone gathers no moss.' You may have lots of friends, but do you ever accomplish anything other than talk? Talk is cheap. How about doing something with your life? You have started lots of projects, but have you ever finished any of them?"

Problems with Pace and Priorities

Have you ever been frustrated with another person's behavior, as illustrated in these two scenes? Have you ever wondered how some people arrive at the conclusions they do? There are two main reasons why people become irritated with each other's behavior, and both reasons relate to social styles. The first reason is pace. People think and move at different paces. Some people operate at a slower pace, carefully plotting and planning before acting. Other people think and move at a faster pace, acting and responding impulsively. Slower paced people often feel uncomfortable with those who act first and think second. Faster paced people are often annoyed by those who are indecisive and slow to act. A faster paced person and a slower paced person will each look at the same circumstances through entirely different eyes.

Pace is the biggest source of friction and conflict between askers (Analyticals and Amiables) and tellers (Drivers and Expressives). Askers are slower paced and tellers are faster paced. The thinking process of Analyticals and Amiables is slow, methodical and step-by-step—deductive. The thinking process of Drivers and Expressives is more intuitive and immediate. Those who think deductively do not understand intuitive thinking. And those who think intuitively have little patience with those who think deductively.

The second reason why people become irritated with each other's behavior is priorities. Some people regard tasks as more important than relationships. Others prioritize relationships over tasks. Who's right and who's

Pace & Priority Problems[1]

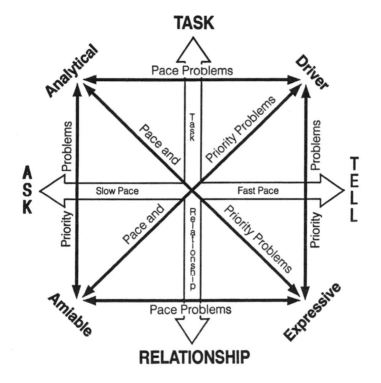

(7-A)

wrong? Is one more important than the other? It all depends on the person you're talking to.

The issue of priorities is the biggest point of contention between task-oriented styles (Analyticals and Drivers) and relationship-oriented styles (Amiables and Expressives). A constant rub exists between those who want to achieve and accomplish and those who want to relate.

The Pace and Priorities Problems chart illustrates the potential conflicts which face the four social styles (see illustration 7-A).

You will notice from the chart that:

- Analyticals and Drivers get along well because both are task-oriented; their conflicts are in the area of pace;
- Amiables and Expressives get along well because both are relationship-oriented; their conflicts are in the area of pace;
- Analyticals and Amiables get along well because both are askers, employing deductive thinking; they rub each other raw in the area of priorities;
- Drivers and Expressives get along well because both are tellers, thinking intuitively; they rub each other raw in the area of priorities;
- Analyticals and Expressives can have larger problems getting along because they clash over both pace and priorities;
- Drivers and Amiables can have larger problems getting along because they clash over both pace and priorities.

A major part of learning to get along with someone is understanding his perspective on life. It takes effort and energy, but when I begin to see situations through the eyes of another person, my compassion develops. I am slower at judging intentions. I can more easily love as Christ loved. The following contrasts in pace and priorities between social styles will help you see life through the eyes of someone different from you:

Pace Conflicts

Askers:
Analyticals and Amiables:

Tellers:
Drivers and Expressives

1. Cannot live life until they understand it
2. Discuss pertinent facts
3. Dislike new problems
4. Attitude reserved and questioning
5. Apply experience to problems
6. Enjoy using skills already learned more than learning new ones
7. Minds inwardly directed—world of ideas and understanding
8. Like to read the fine print
9. Work steadily
10. The people of ideas and abstract invention

1. Cannot understand life until they have lived it
2. Discuss new possibilities
3. Like solving problems
4. Attitude relaxed and confident
5. Apply ingenuity to problems
6. Enjoy learning new skills more than using them
7. Minds outwardly directed—world of people
8. Like to read the signs of coming age
9. Work with bursts of energy
10. The people of action and practical achievement

11. Notice what needs attention now

11. Likes to prepare for the future

12. Reach conclusions step by step

12. Reach conclusions quickly

13. Those who consider, then do, then back to considering

13. Those who do, then consider, then back to doing

14. Have patience; low on enthusiasm

14. Have enthusiasm; low on patience

15. Not often inspired; rarely trust inspiration

15. Follow their inspirations whether good or bad

16. Governed by subjective values

16. Governed by objective conditions

17. Keep track of essential details

17. Look for new essentials

18. Seldom make errors of fact

18. Frequently make errors of fact

19. Subtle and impenetrable

19. Understandable and accessible

20. Face difficulties with realism

20. Tackle difficulties with zest

21. Tend to be good at precise work

21. Dislike taking time for precision

22. Tend to be careful with details; dislike sweeping statements

22. Tend to be faster; dislike complicated procedures

23. Intense and passionate

23. Expansive and less impassioned

24. Do not mind working on one project for long time; routine is okay

24. Often impatient and restless with long, slow jobs; routine is not okay

25. Weakness: tendency toward impracticality

25. Weakness: tendency toward intellectual superficiality

26. Interested in ideas
27. Like quiet and concentration
28. Think before acting
29. Comfortable with little change

26. Interested in results
27. Like variety and action

28. Act before thinking
29. Uncomfortable with lack of variety

Priorities Conflicts

Task-oriented:
Analyticals and Drivers

Relationship-oriented:
Amiables and Expressives

1. Value logic above sentiment
2. Truthful rather than tactful
3. Like to organize
4. Strong executive abilities
5. Question conclusions
6. Brief and businesslike
7. Hurt feelings without knowing it
8. Organize facts; no repetition
9. Like analysis and can live without harmony
10. Tend to decide impersonally

1. Value sentiment above logic
2. Tactful rather than truthful
3. Like to conciliate
4. Strong social abilities
5. Accept conclusions
6. Not brief, but friendly
7. Enjoy pleasing most people
8. Rambles; much repetition
9. Like harmony; badly disturbed by feuds
10. Tend to be influenced in decision

11. Ignore feelings; like facts	11. Ignore facts; like feelings
12. Like to find flaws in advance	12. Like to forecast how others will feel
13. Able to reprimand and fire people when necessary	13. Dislike telling people unpleasant things
14. Tend to be firm-minded	14. Tend to be sympathetic
15. Guard spouses' neglected and unreasonable thinking	15. Guard spouses' neglected and undeveloped thinking
16. Comfortable with ideas	16. Comfortable with people
17. Observant at the expense of imagination	17. Imaginative at the expense of observation
18. Guard emotions	18. Unload emotions
19. Live according to plans	19. Live according to the moment
20. More decisive than curious	20. More curious than decisive
21. Like to have matters decided	21. Like to have decisions open
22. Aim to be right	22. Aim to miss nothing
23. Pleasure in finishing projects	23. Pleasure in starting projects
24. Crave inspiration	24. Crave enjoyment
25. Rational; depend on reasoned judgments	25. Empirical; depend on readiness for anything
26. Generally restless	26. Generally contented
27. Prefer the joy of enterprise and achievement	27. Prefer the art of living in the present

28. Regard feelers as aimless drifters	28. Regard thinkers as half alive
29. Self-regimented, purposeful, exacting	29. Flexible, adaptable, tolerant
30. Need to be treated fairly	30. Need appreciation and praise
31. Contribute to public welfare through inventiveness, initiative, enterprise and inspired leadership	31. Contribute to public welfare through support of every form of enjoyment, recreation, comfort, luxury and beauty[2]

As you have read through the conflicts in pace and priorities, have you been thinking about the conflicts you experience with your loved ones? Are you beginning to realize that the other people in your life do not necessarily see things as you see them? It's easy for us to think about how others rub us the wrong way, how they hurt us. But now that you better understand how the social styles complement and conflict, you can shift your focus from their offensive behavior to your attitudes and actions of response.

Has it dawned on you that other people may be struggling with your thinking and behavior as it is expressed through your social style? Is it possible that you have been acting selfishly, unwilling to admit that you have been wrong? Has your stubbornness and inflexibility destroyed relationships? Have your harsh words hurt those who are closest to you, those you love? Are you in conflict with someone right now? Are you rubbing someone the wrong way?

Maybe you are thinking about someone with whom you have an unresolved conflict. Isn't it about time that you settled your differences? Don't put it off. Both of you have suffered enough hurt. You cannot change the other person, but you can change your response to him. Don't wait for him to make the first move. Be aggressive and try to out-love him.

Take a moment to pray right now. Ask God to forgive you for your selfishness. Ask Him for courage, wisdom and the creativity you need to bridge the conflict gap with your family members, co-workers or fellow church members. God can use you as a mighty minister of healing love if you will let Him. Will you let Him use you?

CHAPTER EIGHT

Reach Out and Meet Someone's Needs

"I don't appreciate you one bit! I think you are wrong. I think you don't care about others. You have no right to do what you are doing."

I was shocked as my friend, speaking over the phone, began to let me have it. Jack had completely misinterpreted my actions, and he proceeded to tell me off in grand fashion for about five minutes. I must confess that my first thoughts were to defend myself and retaliate. But I couldn't get a word in edgeways, so I just listened.

As he began to slow down, I asked, "Is there anything else, Jack?" Jack continued to unload for another two minutes. Then I said, "Is there anything else?" and he went on a minute more. I repeated, "Is there anything else?" Jack was suddenly silent.

After a long pause, Jack said, "You're not responding to me and to what I've said."

"That's right, Jack," I replied. "You have been very

emotional as you have told me what you believe is wrong. You are entitled to your emotions, and I respect your right to give your opinion. But do you have any questions to ask me about the situation?"

At my encouragement, Jack asked a series of questions. After about 15 minutes of questions and answers Jack finally admitted, "Bob, I've really misjudged you. Will you forgive me?"

"Yes," I answered. The conversation continued for a few more minutes, then concluded. The entire episode took about 40 minutes, and we said good-bye as friends. But I was emotionally wrung out, and it took some time for me to clear Jack's strong statements from my mind. Jack had formed some opinions and yielded to some emotions which provoked him to attack me with his back-against-the-wall behavior. Had I been hostile in my response to Jack's attack, we might not be friends today.

Responding Responsibly

It's not easy to demonstrate love in the face of criticism or rejection from others. But we must respond lovingly to others even when we don't feel like it. I've had people tell me, "If I act loving when I don't feel loving, I'd be a hypocrite." No, you are not a hypocrite. Rather, you are a responsible person demonstrating responsible behavior.

If we waited to perform loving activities until we felt like doing them, there would be a lot of neglected activities. For example, when my children were young, I did not feel like changing dirty diapers or getting up in the middle of the night to care for a sick child. Those were loving deeds performed apart from loving feelings. And I don't always feel like going to work, especially when I am sick. Am I a hypocrite because I go to work when I don't feel like it? No, I am a responsible person doing what needs to be done.

When it comes to getting along with people, there are times when we must respond to people in a loving way, not because we feel like doing so, but because it is the loving thing to do. An individual with a heart of love is willing to adapt his behavior to meet the needs and concerns of others, no matter how he feels about doing so. Love seeks to reduce the stress and tension caused by back-against-the-wall behaviors. For example, love will stimulate us to increase our normal pace to meet the needs of a faster paced person. Love will also help us exercise patience and slow our normal pace to meet the needs of slower paced persons. If you are normally task-oriented, love can help you become more aware of the relationship needs of others. Love will help you set aside your strong need for achievement in order to help others feel accepted. And if you are a relationship-oriented person, love will give you the strength and determination to accomplish tasks and duties when you would rather talk to people.

Love seeks for unity between the social styles. Love helps us understand that others have different thinking processes and viewpoints than we do. Love gives us the ability to adapt to the differences in others. Love looks for productive interchange and cooperation.

We do not need to negate our own personalities or deny our own social styles to perform acts of true love. Love helps us magnify the positive characteristics of our social styles. Love helps us exercise behaviors that are not normally dominant in our social styles. Nor does performing activities of love for others mean that we give up our personal goals. On the contrary, we try to reach our goals by adapting our social styles in order to make others feel more comfortable.

Don't Be a Phony

When talking about changing behavior to reduce tension and make others feel comfortable, we must again touch on personal motivation. It is possible for me to modify my behavior and reduce tension, not from a heart of love, but from selfish motives. For example, I may laugh at the boss's jokes, even though they're not funny, so he will like me and help advance my career. This is not love and concern; it's manipulation. We all know how to change our behavior to manipulate, exploit, use or control others.

Instead, our motivation for responsible behavior change must be true love and real concern for others. Loving deeds from a positive motive will be marked by sensitivity, respect, integrity, honesty, understanding, harmony and communication.

The apostle Paul is a good example of someone who adapted personal behavior from positive motivation:

> For though I am free from all men, I have made myself a slave to all, that I might win the more. And to the Jews I became as a Jew, that I might win Jews; to those who are under the Law, as under the Law, though not being myself under the Law, that I might win those who are under the Law; to those who are without law, as without law, though not being without the law of God but under the law of Christ, that I might win those who are without law. To the weak I became weak, that I might win the weak; I have become all things to all men, that I may by all means save some. And I do all things for the sake of the gospel, that I may become a fellow-partaker of it (1 Cor. 9:19-23).

Paul wanted to find common ground with people so that the message of God would not be hindered. To do this he became a slave, one who gives up his rights to please another. That's what adapting behavior is all about. It means giving up the characteristics of my social style to meet the needs of the social styles of others. It is an act of servantlike love.

The ultimate model for adapting behavior is Jesus Christ. Paul commended this model to the Philippian church when he challenged them to focus on the importance of meeting the needs of others:

> Do nothing from selfishness or empty conceit, but with humility of mind let each of you regard one another as more important than himself; do not merely look out for your own personal interests, but also for the interests of others. Have this attitude in yourselves which was also in Christ Jesus, who, although He existed in the form of God, did not regard equality with God a thing to be grasped, but emptied Himself, taking the form of a bond-servant, and being made in the likeness of men. And being found in appearance as a man, He humbled Himself by becoming obedient to the point of death, even death on a cross (Phil. 2:3-8).

My goals for adapting my behavior are to glorify God and love my neighbors. Practically speaking, I must purposely reach out to those of other social styles and meet their needs, even if it means giving up some of my needs. Loving equals giving (see illustration 8-A).

Each Style Must Reach Out

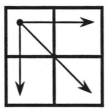

ANALYTICAL

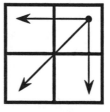

DRIVER

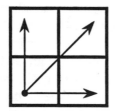

AMIABLE

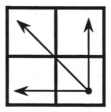

EXPRESSIVE

Adapting to Meet the Needs of Analyticals

1. Analyticals are askers, and they don't appreciate people who come on too strong. Speak softly and slowly to Analyticals.
2. Analyticals are more task-oriented, and they appreciate discussions about achievement. Talk to them about reachable goals.
3. Analyticals are deductive thinkers. Be sure to meet their needs for facts, data, time-lines and step-by-step procedures.
4. Don't expect quick decisions from Analyticals. Give them time to reflect on information before they decide.
5. Analyticals want to know how things work. They appreciate detailed instruction.
6. Analyticals have a strong need to be right and to make right decisions. They would rather make no decision than a wrong decision. Help them realize that it is impossible to make perfect decisions all the time. Help them relax and encourage them during the decision-making process.
7. Analyticals sometimes feel awkward in relationships. Help them save face by not putting too much pressure on them in social situations.
8. Exercise patience when dealing with Analyticals. When they talk, they often give out more information than necessary. They will explain their positions with great detail. Their presentations of material may be so loaded with facts that they are boring and difficult to follow. They have a strong need to explain themselves clearly and completely. You may need to listen to more material than you

would like in order to assure Analyticals that you are listening and that you care.

9. Don't try to oversell your ideas or overstate your positions to Analyticals. They have a strong sense of logic and they can quickly identify reasonable facts. Be clear and specific.

10. Encourage and praise Analyticals for their wise planning, efficient techniques and conservative nature.

Adapting to Meet the Needs of Drivers

1. Drivers are tellers, and they appreciate people who make their points clearly and concisely. Try not to bore them with a lot of details. Get to your bottom line quickly.

2. Drivers are intuitive thinkers and will trust their hunches. Don't try to give them a big sales pitch. If your ideas or suggestions seem valid, Drivers will immediately accept them. However, they may not admit the validity of your ideas because they feel a need to remain in control.

3. Since Drivers like to feel in control, let them choose their methods or paths of response. Tell them the goal you would like to achieve and give them options or alternatives for reaching that goal. But let them use the information to chart their own course.

4. Drivers want to know what is going on, what needs to be accomplished and what your ideas are. They are interested in the answers to how, who, why and when questions. Be sure to let them know what your expectations are. They will tell you if they can or will reach them.

5. Drivers struggle with impatience. Since they pro-

cess information and accomplish tasks quickly, they do not have much patience with those who think or work slowly. Try to increase your pace around Drivers. They appreciate saving time because they want to get on to their many other tasks.

6. Since Drivers move at such a quick pace, try to keep your relationships with them businesslike. If Drivers seem a little cold and matter-of-fact, try not to take it personally. They are more concerned with accomplishments and achievements than with relationships. They look for results.

7. Encourage and praise Drivers for all the jobs and tasks they get done. But don't overdo the encouragement, because they will be off and running to accomplish more before you finish your statement of appreciation.

Adapting to Meet the Needs of Amiables

1. Amiables are askers, and they most appreciate those who are gentle and not brash.

2. Amiables do not offer hasty opinions or make quick decisions, because they don't want to say anything which might hamper their relationships. Help them realize that sharing their thoughts will not affect their relationship with you.

3. Amiables ask, "Why?" They need information that will explain the reasons why they should do something. Explain to them why they need to put forth the effort on a particular task. Help them see how they will benefit from it and how their participation will help everyone else.

4. Amiables have a hard time relaxing in social situations. They don't want to say or do anything that

might cause tension among people. Encourage them that a disagreement with someone is not the end of the world. Help them realize that it is possible for people to hold different opinions and yet remain friends.

5. Amiables do not like to work alone. They need much encouragement and assurance, and they need to feel that they are part of the team. Let them work with you.

6. Amiables like to know that they are accepted. Take time to show personal interest in them.

7. Amiables are hesitant to share their opinions. Learn to be patient in communicating with them. Try not to disagree with them in public or when you suspect that a disagreement will hurt their feelings. Otherwise they will close up and not share anything with you.

8. In order to get Amiables to participate, clearly define what you expect from them. Also communicate to them what you will do to contribute to the relationship or the task at hand.

9. Encourage and praise Amiables with warm personal thanks for their contributions and participation.

Adapting to Meet the Needs of Expressives

1. Expressives are tellers, and they appreciate people who will listen to them and share with them. Become involved with their interests as much as possible.

2. Expressives are intuitive thinkers. They process information and form judgments and opinions quickly. They will also share their opinions openly. Have patience with their quick decisions. They will

operate at a feeling level and may not always be able to give you a rational explanation for their behavior. Have patience with their quick decisions.

3. Expressives have a tendency to "tell it like it is." Try not to take their comments personally. Many times they are simply letting off steam, and you may just happen to be in the way.

4. Expressives are relationship-oriented, and they want to know who is going to be involved. Try to meet their needs for excitement and interaction with people.

5. Expressives tend to start many jobs and not complete them. Try to work with them to accomplish tasks. They like to visit with other people while working, and they do not do their best when working alone.

6. Expressives tend to exaggerate and overgeneralize. Be alert to, and patient with, their overstatements.

7. Expressives become easily sidetracked. Try to help them complete the tasks they start. They like to anticipate the future. Help them become excited about what lies ahead.

8. Encourage and praise Expressives for their enthusiasm. Publicly recognize them and appreciate them for jobs well done.

Learning to adapt my social style to fit the needs of other social styles is a practical expression of loving my neighbor as myself. As I become more open and sensitive to the leading of the Holy Spirit, He will help me lovingly meet the needs of others.

LEARNING TO SHARPEN THE FOCUS OF MY ABILITY TO ADAPT IN LOVE TO THE NEEDS OF OTHERS[1]

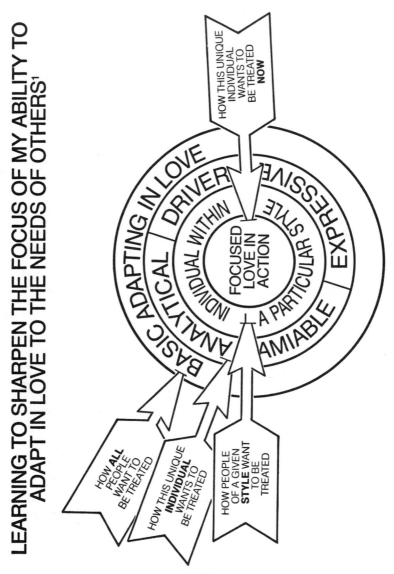

BASIC ADAPTING IN LOVE

DRIVER

EXPRESSIVE

AMIABLE

ANALYTICAL

INDIVIDUAL WITHIN A PARTICULAR STYLE

FOCUSED LOVE IN ACTION

HOW THIS UNIQUE INDIVIDUAL WANTS TO BE TREATED **NOW**

HOW **ALL** PEOPLE WANT TO BE TREATED

HOW THIS UNIQUE **INDIVIDUAL** WANTS TO BE TREATED

HOW PEOPLE OF A GIVEN **STYLE** WANT TO BE TREATED

(8-B)

CHAPTER NINE

Loving with Style

Carl and Cheryl first met at a party at the Johnson's home. Cheryl arrived a little early and helped Peggy Johnson with last minute preparations. The party had been underway for some time when Cheryl heard a commotion at the front door. Soon she understood what the noise and excitement was all about: A young man named Carl had arrived. He was very outgoing and friendly. His laughter seemed to brighten the room. He was soon the life of the party.

Carl circulated through the crowd and met everyone there, including Cheryl. They were attracted to each other somehow, and the attraction seemed deeper than physical appearance. Cheryl liked Carl's happy-go-lucky, carefree spirit. She admired the way he could approach strangers and turn them into friends. Carl noticed how Cheryl spent quality time with one or two people at the party. He could tell that she was very sensitive and caring. Carl's winning smile and creative spirit won him a date with Cheryl.

They had a wonderful time on their date. They went to the craziest places in town, places Cheryl would never have gone on her own. She never laughed so hard on a date before. And Carl had the best time of his life. He had never met anyone as interesting as Cheryl. She was well read and kept up with current events. Her natural beauty was enhanced by the way she dressed. She looked like a model who had just stepped off the cover of a fashion magazine. Not too many months passed before Carl and Cheryl were married.

They began to experience a little conflict right from the start of the honeymoon. It wasn't anything big. Cheryl was a little irritated that Carl squeezed the toothpaste tube in the middle and left the cap off. But she put the cap back on and rolled the tube up from the end.

As the months rolled by, Carl and Cheryl experienced more and more conflict. Cheryl's attraction to Carl's happy-go-lucky spirit cooled as he became increasingly carefree in his use of the checkbook. He threw his clothes on the floor instead of the hamper, and was late for appointments, especially dinner. Meanwhile, Carl's fascination with Cheryl's neatness and grooming diminished when he began to see her as a picky perfectionist. There was trouble brewing in their home.

Opposites Attract

People like Carl and Cheryl don't realize that a man and a woman are often attracted to each other by positive personality traits which are the opposite of their own. Usually, it isn't until after the honeymoon that they discover the negative side which exists for the strengths they admire in their partners. That which fascinates and attracts at first can in time irritate and bother. For this reason, many couples endure marriage with kind of a love/hate relationship, confessing, "I can't live with him/her and I can't live without him/her."

One of the biggest conflicts in any marriage occurs between the social styles of the husband and wife. If partners could understand the differences between social styles, and learn to accept each other and not try to change each other, we would see the divorce rate in our country and in our churches decline. As we look at the various combinations of marriages between social styles, think about your parents' marriage. What were their individual social styles? What were/are the strengths and weaknesses of their marriage? Where were/are their conflict points? If you are married, examine your own marriage in light of the strengths and weaknesses of the combinations described in this chapter. If you are dating, try to imagine the possible future conflicts you may experience with your dating partner based on your social styles.

When an Analytical Marries a Driver

Alan is an Analytical and Amy is a Driver. Alan and Amy work in the yard together. If you saw their home, you would be impressed with how nice their yard looks compared to others in the neighborhood. They seem to work well with each other because they both want a well-kept home.

But once in awhile Alan and Amy clash over how the yard work is to be done. Alan wants to do the work in a step-by-step way while Amy just wants to hurry and get it done. If Amy had her way, they could keep the yard looking fine without spending so much time on minor details. There are many other projects Amy would like them to work on beside the yard. But Alan does not like to start a project unless he can do it right. He spends a good deal of time making sure that the grass is mowed in different directions and that the flower beds are laid out in very straight lines.

Analytical/Driver marriages usually work well because both partners are task-oriented. This couple will accomplish much because both have a very strong work ethic. They will blend well because of their mutual inclination toward accomplishment, reaching goals and finishing jobs (see illustration 9-A).

The Analytical/Driver couple will conflict in the area of pace. Analyticals are slower paced and more precise than Drivers. Drivers don't care as much about details and perfection; they just want to get the job done. For the Driver, the more jobs completed, the better, even if they are not polished to perfection. A Driver will struggle with his Analytical partner's hesitancy in making decisions. *Drivers* make quick, intuitive decisions while Analyticals make slower, deductive decisions. Neither understands the thinking process of the other, nor do they have much patience with how the other approaches conclusions.

When an Analytical Marries an Amiable
Larry is an Amiable and Lori is an Analytical. Larry is a very gentle and calm person. Nothing seems to bother him very much. He gets along with everyone. Lori is on the quiet and reserved side. She likes to stay at home working on crafts and spending lots of time with the children.

Larry and Lori never seem to have any major disagreements. The only thing that bothers Larry a little is that he would like to spend more time with other couples. He doesn't mind being home in the evenings playing with the children, but he would like to go out more often. Lori gets a little upset with Larry because he is always the last

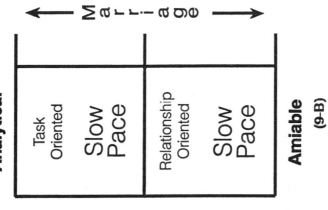

Analytical

Task Oriented
Slow Pace

Relationship Oriented
Slow Pace

Amiable

← M a r r i a g e →

(9-B)

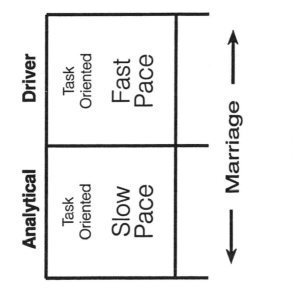

Analytical

Task Oriented
Slow Pace

Driver

Task Oriented
Fast Pace

← Marriage →

(9-A)

one to leave a party. She attends social gatherings, but likes to leave earlier than Larry does. Lori thinks that Larry has a tendency to be a little lazy. She has a hard time getting him to do things around the house. Larry wishes that Lori would loosen up a little and not be so bound by schedules.

Amiables and Analyticals do well in their marriages because both partners are askers, slower paced, polite in their communication and not usually aggressive with each other. They have mutual respect for each other's rights (see illustration 9-B).

The Amiable/Analytical couple conflicts in the area of priorities. Amiables are more relationship-oriented and Analyticals are more task-oriented. There will be a continual rub between the one who is more time- and goal-conscious and the one who is more casual, and who enjoys spending large blocks of time with people. Both Analyticals and Amiables think deductively. But the Analytical will approach decisions by looking at the facts, while the Amiable will approach the same decisions by looking at how they will affect people.

When an Amiable Marries an Expressive

Ted is an Amiable and Tracy is an Expressive. Ted and Tracy are always on the go. They love doing things with their friends. They enjoy having many people in their home. They are actively involved in church and community functions. They attend all of their children's athletic events, cheering them on energetically from the sidelines. No one is a stranger to Ted and Tracy.

Tracy is the life of the party. She is very outgoing, warm and enthusiastic. She loves life and squeezes as much of it as possible out of every experience. Ted is easygoing, very supportive and has a dry sense of humor.

Ted wishes that Tracy would slow down a little. He has a hard time keeping up with her constant activity. He likes Tracy's outgoing nature, but he thinks that she sometimes stretches the truth. He worries about what others think of her propensity for exaggeration and excitability. Tracy doesn't think that Ted has any solid opinions. She sees him as a conformer, not standing up for his rights. She feels like she is always dragging information out of him.

Amiables and Expressives do well in their marriages because they are both relationship-oriented. They both enjoy being with people. They like to talk about most anything. They are very friendly and usually well-liked. They have mutual respect for each other because of their involvement with people (see illustration 9-C).

The Amiable/Expressive couple will conflict in the area of pace. Amiables are deductive thinkers and will analyze how their decisions affect others. Expressives are intuitive thinkers and will make decisions on the spur of the moment and without much regard for others. The Amiable mate does not like the fact that his Expressive partner's quick decisions often hurt others. The Expressive spouse is impatient with the Amiable who can never make up his mind, always drags his feet and often throws cold water on his ideas.

When an Expressive Marries a Driver

Dan is an Expressive and Deborah is a Driver. Dan is very ambitious and charismatic. He is a good salesman on the job and with his family. He is lots of fun and likes to do things that are unique and different. Deborah is a very protective woman who is willing to change and try new things. She is very practical and does not have much trouble making decisions. Both Dan and Deborah are strongly opinionated and are open to sharing their opinions. They

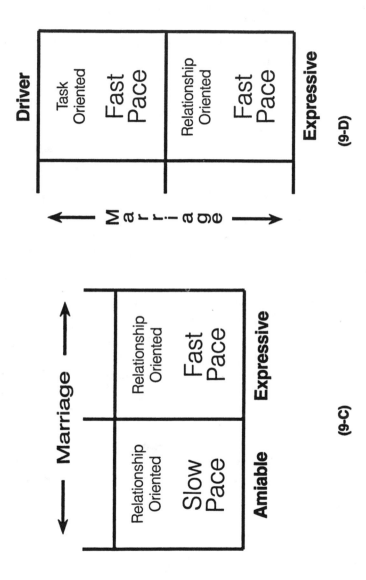

Driver

| Task Oriented Fast Pace | Relationship Oriented Fast Pace |

Marriage

Expressive

(9-D)

Marriage

| Relationship Oriented Slow Pace | Relationship Oriented Fast Pace |

Amiable   **Expressive**

(9-C)

like the fact that they can both talk about issues with firm convictions.

Deborah sometimes thinks that Dan does a lot more talking than working. She wishes that he would finish the projects he starts, especially cleaning up the garage. Dan thinks that Deborah needs to relax and not always be on the run. He does not like the fact that she won't do things on the spur of the moment. He sometimes thinks that Deborah is like a Marine drill sergeant.

Expressives and Drivers do well in their marriages because they are both tellers. Each partner always knows where he stands with the other. They are both intuitive thinkers and comprehend quickly. They are both faster paced and make decisions without delay. (See illustration 9-D.)

The Expressive/Driver couple will clash in the area of priorities. Drivers are more task-oriented and Expressives are more relationship-oriented. Expressives do not like the seemingly cold, matter-of-fact, businesslike nature of Drivers. Drivers do not like the "all talk and no action" behavior of Expressives. Drivers think that Expressives are weak-willed, disorganized and undependable.

Crisscross Marriages: Double Trouble

When two people marry representing crisscross social styles (Analytical/Expressive or Amiable/Driver), they face two major problems: pace and priorities (see illustration 9-E).

This is not to say that all crisscross marriages will not survive. Many of them will. However, crisscross marriages face more difficult conflicts than the other combinations mentioned which have only one conflict area. This explains why some marriages struggle more than others.

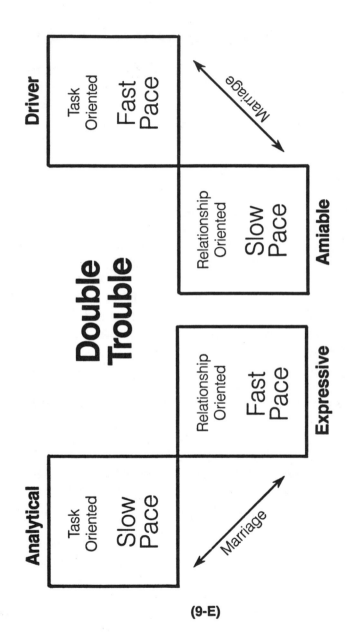

(9-E)

There is one crisscross marriage combination which may be in for triple trouble, especially when the partners are Christians. It's the Driver/Amiable combination with the Driver being the wife. Not only will this couple face pace and priorities problems, but the wife may have problems submitting to her husband, who is not the natural leader that she is. The wife who is a Driver must temper her own social style and make difficult changes in her behavior in order to wait for her husband to decide and lead. Since she is a teller and a decision-maker, it may be very difficult for her to adapt to her slower paced, less aggressive husband.

We Don't Need Clones

The tendency in marriage is for each partner to try to remake his spouse into his own image. We try to get them to think the way we think. We try to teach them to make decisions the way we make them. We urge them to speed up or slow down to match our pace. We push them to adapt the same task-orientation or relationship-orientation we prefer. We tend to forget what made our partners attractive to us in the first place: their difference. If we were all Analyticals our households would be well-organized, but we probably wouldn't have much fun or excitement. Think what would happen if we were all Drivers. We would have no followers to control. If we were all Amiables we would have a peaceful world, but no one would make any decisions or have much enthusiasm for life. And if the world contained only Expressives we would have a lot of fun, but it's doubtful that anyone would accomplish much.

When we try to change another person from the outside, we tend to destroy that person. We need to accept people—especially our mates—the way they are. That's what Jesus did. And if there is negative behavior which needs to be changed—and we all have some—we need to allow God to change our partners from the inside out. Sometimes we usurp the responsibility of being the change agent which rightfully belongs to the Holy Spirit. Instead, we need to relax and trust that God is in control. We need to focus on living godly lives ourselves, changing our behavior where it needs to be changed and adapting our social styles to meet the needs of our partners. We need to develop tolerance, mutual caring, love and understanding (see 1 Cor. 12:18-19; Eph. 4:16).

What Destroys a Marriage?

As a Marriage, Family and Child Counselor with thousands of hours of counseling experience, I am convinced that it's not the big problems in life that destroy marriages. Major tragedies like the death of a child, a house burning down or a flood usually pull families together. Rather, it's the little things that tear relationships apart:

- who forgot to shut the door?
- who left bread crumbs on the butter dish?
- who smeared peanut butter in the jelly?
- whose turn is it to wash the dishes, carry out the trash, do the laundry or mow the lawn?
- why didn't you hang up the wet towel?
- why didn't you fill the gas tank after using the car?
- why can't you balance the checkbook?
- why don't you know what my needs are?

Individually, these behaviors are minor and silly, and none of them seem capable of destroying a marriage. But the small irritations of life are like bricks which slowly build up to produce a wall which keeps two people from knowing and loving each other.

The Wall

Their wedding picture mocked them from the table, these two, whose minds no longer touched each other.

They lived with such a heavy barricade between them that neither battering ram of words nor artilleries of touch could break it down.

Somewhere, between the oldest child's first tooth and the youngest daughter's graduation, they lost each other.

Throughout the years, each slowly unraveled that tangled ball of string called self, and as they tugged at stubborn knots each hid his searching from the other.

Sometimes she cried at night and begged the whispering darkness to tell her who she was.

He lay beside her, snoring like a hibernating bear, unaware of her winter.

Once, after they had made love, he wanted to tell her how afraid he was of dying, but, fearing to show his naked soul, he spoke instead about the beauty of her breasts.

She took a course in modern art, trying to find herself in colors splashed upon a canvas, and complained to other women about men who were insensitive.

He climbed into a tomb called "the office,"
    wrapped his mind in a shroud of paper
    figures and buried himself in customers.
Slowly, the wall between them rose, cemented
    by the mortar of indifference.
One day, reaching out to touch each other, they
    found a barrier they could not pene-
    trate, and recoiling from the coldness of
    the stone, each retreated from the
    stranger on the other side.
For when love dies . . . it is not in a moment of
    angry battle . . . nor when fiery bodies
    lose their heat.
It lies panting . . . exhausted . . . expiring at
    the bottom of a wall it could not scale.[1]

How Do You Put a Marriage Together Again?

In order to put a troubled marriage back together again, you need to put five steps into operation:

Step one: "I'm sorry." Before you can say, "I'm sorry," you must acknowledge that there is a problem in the first place. Acknowledging the problems doesn't mean deciding which partner is smart and which is dumb, which is strong and which is weak, or which is right and which is wrong. Rather, it means acknowledging regret for actions or words which have caused someone else to hurt.

But sorrow is only the starting point, not the finishing point. Spurgeon, the great preacher, said, "Sorrow pays no debt." Being sorry does not replace a broken vase, repair a damaged car or heal an emotional wound caused by harsh words. Sorrow cannot take away a pregnancy or bring back to life a person killed by a drunk driver. Sorrow only indicates that a person realizes a conflict exists and wishes the problem had never occurred. Sorrow is the place to begin. As one becomes aware of the clash brought about by differing social styles and insensitive behaviors in the marriage, only then will the stage be set for change. One must come to the place where he realizes that his social style behavior is causing discomfort to his mate.

Step two: "I've been wrong." If you think saying, "I'm sorry" is hard, try saying, "I've been wrong." To admit you are wrong means eating crow. Barbecued, fried, mashed, stewed or anyway you serve it, crow is difficult to eat. Admitting you are wrong is an act of repentance. It means that you feel sorrow deeply enough to change. It is only when behavior changes that hurt begins to heal. Admitting that we are wrong is humbling, not something we like to do. It means admitting that we are not perfect. But it will help motivate us to positive behavior. It is painful enough to drive home the point that we are responsible for our behavior.

Step three: "Please forgive me." When you realize that there is trouble in your marriage relationship, and you feel the sorrow and regret of the tension and conflict, and you acknowledge that your attitudes, actions or words have been wrong, you are then ready for healing. Forgiveness brings about healing. Although your partner may say he forgives you for hurting him, he is the one who gets healed. By asking forgiveness you open the door for the salve of repentance and changed behavior to heal his wound. It is a gracious thing to forgive. It is also a gracious thing to bring healing to a wounded partner by asking for forgiveness.

Do you care enough about the mate you have hurt to bring healing and life to him or her? Ask God to help you put aside any pride, and go to your partner now. Don't let the wound continue to bleed. Even if you have been wounded yourself, reach out in your pain. The process will heal both of you.

Step four: "I love you." For broken relationships to be healed, both parties must be plunged into a fountain of love. True love does not reside only in words; it finds its power in actions. True love must be demonstrated through actions, even when you don't feel like it.

When couples come to me for marriage counseling, it is not uncommon for one or both of the partners to say, "I don't feel like I love him anymore." I never argue the point. I believe they are telling the truth—they really do feel that their love has died. Rather, I smile and ask, "Would you like to feel it again?" The usual reaction is disbelief. Is it possible for love to return? Yes, love can be rekindled, revived and renewed.

The reason couples feel like their love has died is that they have stopped performing loving deeds for each other. Never has a person seeking marriage counseling said to me, "I've got to get out of this marriage because my mate is too good to me. He loves me too much. I can't stand it anymore!" People who lavish loving words and deeds upon one another generously will find their love-fire blazing hot. Two unselfish partners never get a divorce.

Demonstrating love in the context of social styles means moving out of your comfort zone to make your mate feel comfortable—even when you don't feel like it. This is done by moving from the extremes of your social style toward the center. If you are slow paced, speed up, If you are fast paced, slow down. If you are task-oriented, get more involved with people. If you are relationship-oriented, try to accomplish more tasks. Remember, just because your mate is different does not mean that he is less of a person or wrong in his outlook. Learn to see life from his point of view.

You may say, "That's not easy. You don't know my mate." But if I promised to give you $1,000, could you learn to understand your mate's viewpoint? How about $10,000? How about $100,000? Am I getting warm? You see, when the price is right, we can do almost anything we put our minds to. What price would you pay to have a happy marriage? How about spending a little love and concern?

Step five: "Let's try again." To try again means to erase the chalkboard of life and start fresh. We cannot change the past—it's gone. And to rehearse it repeatedly only debilitates us. Reliving the past does not solve anything, remove anything or change anything. We must learn to move on from the past which binds us to hurt and pain. Paul the apostle refers to this concept when he says in Philippians 3:13-15: "Forgetting what lies behind and reaching forward to what lies ahead, I press on toward the goal for the prize of the upward call of God in Christ Jesus. Let us therefore, as many as are perfect, have this attitude." It is good—but not always easy—to "bury the hatchet" and let the bad be forgotten.

When I was a boy, my brother and I fought quite a bit. We often were punished for our actions. My mother used one form of punishment which, to my mind, was the worst form of punishment known to man. It was worse than a spanking, worse than solitary confinement, even worse than having your mouth washed out with soap, standing in the corner or losing your favorite toy. My mother would punish us by making us kiss and make up. Yuk! I would have taken any other punishment over kissing my brother. But it worked. One kiss-and-make-up session kept us from fighting for a long time.

If I had the power, I would make troubled husbands and wives kiss and make up. I know they would not like it at first. They would resist it because nobody likes to kiss the person they are angry at. That's just the point. When you are kissing, you're not fighting. Do you need to forget the past? Do you need to kiss and make up? Go ahead and do it; you won't die from it. God will help you put your marriage back together again. Will you let Him?

CHAPTER TEN
Leading with Style

During a discussion on the topic of leadership, Henry Ford once said, "'Who ought to be the boss?' is like asking, 'Who ought to be the tenor in the quartet?' Obviously, the man who can sing tenor."[1]

Former president Dwight Eisenhower once declared:

> In order to be a leader a man must have followers. And to have followers, a man must have their confidence. Hence the supreme quality for a leader is unquestionable integrity. Without it, no real success is possible, no matter whether it is on a section gang, a football field, in an army, or in an office. If a man's associates find him guilty of phoniness, if they find that he lacks forthright integrity, he will fail. His teachings and actions must square with each other. The first great need, therefore, is integrity and high purpose.[2]

Which social style makes the best leader? It is often assumed that individuals who are more extroverted—the tellers—make better leaders than introverted persons—the askers. Don't rely on this assumption. An outspoken person is not necessarily better qualified for leadership. There is much more to leadership than the ability to state one's opinions well. The exciting thing about the social styles concept is that effective, successful leaders can be found in all four social styles. Every leader will reflect the characteristics of his style—Analytical, Driver, Amiable or Expressive. The most important factors in leadership, regardless of social style, are integrity and purpose. All of the social styles can benefit from the following insights on leadership:

> Don't follow any leader until you know whom he is following . . . . It's extremely difficult to lead farther than you have gone yourself . . . . A good leader inspires men to have confidence in him; a great leader inspires them to have confidence in themselves . . . . The business of a leader is to turn weakness into strength, obstacles into stepping stones, and disaster into triumph . . . . A real leader faces the music even when he dislikes the tune.[3]

> You do not lead by hitting people over the head—that's assault, not leadership (Dwight Eisenhower).[4]

> You can judge a leader by the size of problems he tackles—people nearly always pick a problem their own size, and ignore or leave to oth-

ers the bigger or smaller ones (Anthony Jay) .... No man will ever be a big executive who feels that he must, either openly or under cover, follow up every order he gives and see that it is done—nor will he ever develop a capable assistant (John L. Mahin).[5]

Without wise leadership, a nation is in trouble; but with good counselors there is safety (Prov. 11:14, *TLB*).

The Analytical Leader: The Technique Specialist

Andrew oversees the testing department for a large computer manufacturer. He started with the company when he graduated from college. He has been a very consistent and productive employee. Because of his attention to detail, he was promoted to a level where he now supervises 35 other employees. Andrew, leading from the Analytical social style, has a great many strengths which benefit his employer.

Andrew excels in establishing policies, schedules, routines and procedures for his department. His fellow employees are amazed at all the details he can handle simultaneously. Everyone appreciates Andrew's dependability. He is responsible, perseverative and accurate. He fulfills obligations and keeps his promises and commitments. Andrew's supervisor, Nick, is quite impressed with Andrew's professionalism, self-discipline and logical way of approaching decisions. Nick greatly appreciates Andrew's desire to preserve the traditions of the organization. Andrew has a conservative nature and is cautious about putting his company in any position that might cause a loss of production or efficiency.

Andrew's Analytical style of leadership also has some great weaknesses which can cause problems for his company. On his bad days, Andrew can stir up negative feelings in those who work under him. Sometimes they see him as a walking vacuum cleaner of facts. Andrew often gets so involved in data collection that he doesn't get the job done. Those working under him get frustrated because he shies away from making decisions and taking risks. They complain that his systematic thoroughness turns into picky perfectionism. The employees feel the tension created by Andrew's critical and negative thinking. They think he exaggerates all the possible problems on a project or a decision to be made.

When Andrew gets involved with a task, he often becomes quiet and withdraws from interaction. His employees feel that he is cool, distant and reserved. They dislike his lack of warmth, stern commands and austere actions. They sometimes see him as stuffy and unable to have fun or enjoy close relationships.

Andrew is resistant to change and has the ability to throw cold water on new ideas. Nick realizes that Andrew has a hunger to serve, but he is sometimes confused as to whether Andrew is serving the company or some overpowering drive within himself. Nick wonders if Andrew is trying to pay back some kind of "work debt" to society. Often Nick has to tell Andrew to go home, reminding him that his work will still be there in the morning.

The Driver Leader: The Control Specialist

Brad is self-employed. He worked for another company for several years before deciding to go into business for himself. He has a young, growing company with about 15 employees. Those working under Brad appreciate his independent spirit and the independence he allows them to exercise in their various positions. Brad does not pressure them about details; he is more results-oriented. He is a visionary leader who causes everyone to rise to the challenges and opportunities he sets before them.

Those working directly with Brad appreciate his cool logic, his competitiveness and his willingness to take risks. Because Brad makes decisions easily, everything seems to be at a quick pace in the office. He seems to understand quickly the implications of decisions and problems that come to him on a daily basis. Brad is self-disciplined and driven, and he loves to tackle complex situations and shoot for lofty goals. He is efficient, productive and has become an architect for change in his growing business. Not only can he conceptualize ideas, but he can describe his ideas so colorfully that his subordinates can visualize the end results. Brad's strengths as a Driver leader will carry his company far.

But watch out! When the wind is not blowing in Brad's favor, he can become a human tornado. His pragmatism turns into bossiness and stubbornness. He may make some hasty decisions which get him into trouble. He starts large and complex problems, pushes them to a certain point and then passes them on to others. He does not like to maintain what he starts. Sometimes Brad appears to be restless and unfulfilled.

Brad can sometimes be as cold as ice and as unfeeling as a piece of steel with his employees. He can be tough and cruel. He will display impatience and anger when he must repeat his directives to his troops. He has a hard time with those who complain that he is running over them and demanding too much from them. He will respond, "If you can't stand the heat, get out of the kitchen!" He can become very sarcastic, and he will not tolerate frivolity on the job. The weaknesses of Brad's Driver leadership style have the potential to destroy his company and the people who work for him.

The Amiable Leader: The Support Specialist

Chuck is in charge of the personnel department in an automobile manufacturing plant. He is responsible for hiring employees and attending to their social, educational and personal needs at the plant. Chuck was hired because of his ability to get along with people and make them feel comfortable.

On the positive side of his Amiable leadership, Chuck is very friendly and cooperative in his contact with both the employees and the administrative staff. He has the ability to say the right thing at the right time. He is diplomatic in his dealings with people and has become the spokesman for the organization. He's very patient with employees and is a good listener. He is generous to a fault. He knows how to lubricate communication and give sincere appreciation. He is willingly helpful to others and is a team player. The employees appreciate his supportive, easygoing, loyal nature. He does an excellent job running step-by-step training programs.

On the negative side, Chuck is so nice that it is difficult for anyone to really get angry with him, even though he does provoke frustration in his fellow workers. Sometimes he can be very quiet, shy and retiring. He hates conflict so much that he is often too soft-hearted to discipline employees for misbehavior. He especially resists terminating an employee, putting off the confrontation as long as possible, even if the offending employee is an extra burden for other employees.

Chuck is afraid of hurting anyone's feelings and often finds himself a slave to the priorities of others. Because of his inability to say no, Chuck takes on too many responsibilities and becomes overly tired. Manny, Chuck's supervisor, has noticed that Chuck does not like open-ended schedules. Rather, Chuck seeks detailed structure from Manny and needs lots of strokes and recognition for his accomplishments.

Chuck seems to blame himself for the failures of others. He does not adjust well to change, and he really hates surprises. Chuck seems to be absorbed in a search for self-understanding. Although Chuck's Amiable leadership may not present glaring problems, he can be a real emotional drag on those he works with.

The Expressive Leader: The Social Specialist

David is the advertising manager for a large chain of department stores. David and his staff of ten are responsible for creating ads for newspapers, radio and television. David loves his job. It has lots of variety and is filled with excitement and challenge.

As an Expressive leader, David is very outgoing, enthusiastic and stimulating, and he rarely has a down day. Those working for him appreciate his friendliness, warmth and caring. His company appreciates his optimism, cheerfulness and ability to verbalize appreciation to those working with him. David is spontaneous, talkative and personable, with a flair for the dramatic and the imaginative. He is flashy, competitive, persuasive and fun-loving. He is a bundle of ideas. He could sell ice to Eskimos. He is also a good trouble-shooter in a crisis. He knows how to get people to work together in good spirits. He has a nose for new opportunities and a good sense of timing. David adds zest to his company with the positive traits of his Expressive leadership.

But there is another side to David that is not much fun. At times he can be very loud, obnoxious and downright insulting. If he does not like something, he will let everyone within earshot know it. He is highly emotional, impulsive and excitable. He is slow paced and tends to slow down the whole organization, driving everyone crazy. He sometimes shows up late for appointments, forgets important meetings and keeps customers waiting. He will often make commitments for himself and others that he will not keep. He can be very impatient and rigid when crossed. He is restless and will start far more tasks than he will ever complete. He is easily bored, causing him to shift suddenly to more exciting projects, leaving his staff to pick up the pieces. Sometimes he will create a crisis just so he will have something to do. He hates paperwork and rules, and he will put off unpleasant jobs as long as possible. When David's Expressive leadership goes bad, it goes bad with gusto—and the whole company feels it.

As illustrated above, all four social styles can produce effective leaders or destructive disasters. Each leader must be willing to take an objective look at both the positive and negative sides of his leadership style. Effective leadership for any style involves the process of accentuating positive traits and eliminating negative traits.

Helping Followers Follow

Regardless of your social style, if you are responsible for

others as a leader, you need to be aware of what your subordinates need in order to be productive followers. In order to lead effectively, you must know the unique needs of each follower based on his social style.

Followers Need . . .

Analyticals: . . . reasons why they should participate in or complete tasks.

Drivers: . . . options or alternatives for completing tasks, and freedom to select them.

Amiables: . . . assurance that they will not be left alone to complete tasks.

Expressives: . . . exciting premiums or incentives for completing tasks.

Followers Ask . . .

Analyticals: . . . "How does it work? How is it put together? How do I complete the task?"

Drivers: . . . "What is it? What is your idea or plan? What do you want me to do?"

Amiables: . . . "Why should I do that? Why should I attempt this and risk losing our relationship?"

Expressives: . . . "Who else is involved? Who will I interact with? Who is in charge?"

Followers Want Freedom to . . .

Analyticals: . . . breathe. Let them off the hook. Give them time to think and react—especially in interpersonal relationships.

Drivers: . . . win. Let them choose the most successful paths for reaching the goals you suggest. Give them choices.

Amiables: . . . relax. They already have enough relationship tension in their social style. Don't give them more.

Expressives: . . . gain. They have high aspirations for many relationships. They need endorsement and encouragement.

Followers Are Motivated to Save . . .

Analyticals: . . . face. They feel awkward handling relationships and problems. No decision is better than a wrong decision.

Drivers: . . . time. Time is money. Structure saves time. A bad decision is better than no decision.

Amiables: . . . relationships. They will complete the task, but usually as a result of having preserved relationships.

Expressives: . . . effort. They are sensitive to the complexity of people, and they want shorter and more direct systems for saving effort. They will get the task done through initiating new relationships.

Followers Irritate Others By . . .

Analyticals: . . . expressing negativism and criticism.

Drivers: . . . displaying impatience and sarcasm.

Amiables: . . . not being able to make decisions.

Expressives: . . . not following through.

Followers Are Irritated By . . .

Analyticals: . . . those who do not keep regulations and deadlines.

Drivers: . . . being asked to perform tasks which are illogical or unreasonable.

Amiables: . . . pressure of any kind.

Expressives: . . . rules and procedures.

Followers Need to Learn . . .

Analyticals: . . . to decide. They want to make perfect decisions every time, so they put off making any decisions.

Drivers: . . . to listen. Because of their fast pace, they do not take time to really listen to others and their concerns.

Amiables: . . . to reach. They are so concerned about relationships that they will not attempt anything risky or express their opinions for fear of losing relationships.

Expressives: . . . to check. They have such strong opinions that they make statements without checking the facts. They will make generalizations from a sampling of one.

Followers Need Leaders Who . . .

Analyticals: . . . give suggestions. They need clarification. They like alternatives for implementation. They want practical methods for projects.

Drivers: . . . allow freedom. They need to know clearly what the goal is, and then be allowed the freedom to get the job done their way and at their pace.

Amiables: . . . provide direction. They need to have structure, detailed instructions and much encouragement. They need to understand their relationship to the project as a whole.

Expressives: . . . provide inspiration. They need broad structure, but not detailed methods. They like excitement, encouragement and personal support.

Followers Measure Progress By . . .

Analyticals: . . . activity. They need to be involved with lots of facts, details and projects.

Drivers: . . . results. They need to reach goals and objectives, and accomplish tasks.

Amiables: . . . attention. They need to know that they are noticed and that their work is appreciated.

Expressives: . . . applause. They need to feel loved and know that their contributions are appreciated.

Followers Want Appreciation for Their . . .

Analyticals: . . . carefulness.

Drivers: . . . capabilities.

Amiables: . . . contributions.

Expressives: . . . cleverness.

CHAPTER ELEVEN

A Life Filled with Style

By now you are aware that the helpful implications of social styles in our daily lives and relationships are many and diverse. We have explored social styles at many levels of interpersonal relationships such as conflicts, marriage and leadership. But it is impossible to consider in one book all the implications of this concept. In this final chapter I would like to highlight briefly several additional areas of life where you can apply your understanding of social styles.

Social Styles in the Bible

Sometimes I am asked, "How does the social styles theory relate to the Bible?" The answer is that it relates indirectly rather than directly. The Bible was not written to describe or promote social styles. It was written to convey God's plan of redemption for lost mankind. Social styles theory is basically a description of broad groups of behaviors which fallen men and women—both saved and unsaved—display. The social styles theory helps us understand man's human condition and his interaction with his fellow beings.

If you examine the Scriptures through the eyes of the social styles concept, you will notice that the behavior of Bible characters can be identified by social style. For example, Analytical behavior can been seen in detail-conscious Dr. Luke, in doubting Thomas and in moody Moses. Paul was unquestionably a Driver, as was crafty Jacob and pushy Mrs. Zebedee, the mother of James and John. The Amiable behavior of Abraham is graphic. He gave Lot all the best land to avoid conflict, and he lied about his wife to save his own skin. Amiable behavior is also seen in the quiet resolve of Queen Esther and in the spirit of restoration displayed by Barnabas. The apostle Peter stands out as a prime example of the Expressive. On the negative side, Jezebel is a clear picture of an Expressive displaying back-against-the-wall behavior. And Esau typifies the live-for-the-moment attitude of the Expressive.

Some Bible characters were askers and some were tellers. And the evidence of task-orientation and relationship-orientation can been seen in the following passages: "The Son of Man did not come to be served, but to serve [task], and to give His life a ransom for many [relationship]" (Matt. 20:28); "Having thus a fond affection for you [relationship], we were well-pleased to impart to you [task] not only the gospel of God but also our own lives, because you had become very dear to us [relationship]" (1 Thess. 2:8).

Hopefully, the social styles concept will help you look at Bible characters as real people who faced the same kinds of pressures and conflicts that we encounter. If you would like an in-depth look at several Bible characters and their styles, I suggest Dr. Tim LaHaye's book, *Transformed Temperaments* (Harvest House Publishers).

Taking Your Style to Church

Allow me to pose, and then respond to, four questions which deal with social styles in the life of the local church:

1. Do people's social styles play a role in church splits, disputes and general unrest?
Earlier I suggested that we wrongly attempt to mold others into our own social styles instead of accepting them for the styles they are. Similarly, I think that many church fights and hurt feelings occur because:

- some people think deductively and some people think intuitively;
- some people are "letter of the law" (task-oriented) believers and some people are "spirit of the law" (relationship-oriented) believers;
- some people are slow paced—embracing tradition and sameness—and some people are fast paced—preferring new methods and ideas;
- some people pass off their social style opinions and beliefs as if they were right out of the Bible. "How could anyone think or believe any differently?" they question. "If they do, they are either wrong, mislead or downright sinful."

What would happen if we tried to look at issues in the church from the viewpoint of other social styles? What would happen if we attempted to understand everybody else's point of view?

*2. What would happen if pastors were selected on the basis of
their social styles and the social style needs of congregations?*
In fact, I have wondered if a church takes on an overall
social style. Are there Analytical churches, Driver
churches, Amiable churches and Expressive churches?
What happens when a church switches from a caring Amiable pastor to a task-oriented Driver pastor? Are there
pace and priorities conflicts for the congregation? What
happens when a church replaces a scholarly Analytical pastor with an Expressive pastor who loves people but
doesn't study much? Would the congregation be upset?

I think the social styles concept could change, for the
better, the way a pastoral search committee selects a pastor.

*3. Does the social style of a pastor or Sunday school teacher
affect the way he preaches or teaches?*
Generally speaking, I believe that:

- Analytical pastors and teachers give fact-oriented sermons and lessons;
- Driver pastors and teachers give action-oriented sermons and lessons;
- Amiable pastors and teachers give relationship-
  oriented sermons and lessons;
- Expressive pastors and teachers give excitement-
  oriented sermons and lessons.

If I'm right, it is possible that a pastor or teacher may
be missing the social style needs of 75 percent of his congregation or class. Perhaps it would be wise for pastors
and teachers to plan sermons and lessons which would
attempt to meet the needs of all four social styles by
including:

- facts and evidence for the Analyticals;
- action and goals for the Drivers;
- relationship and caring for the Amiables;
- and excitement and challenge for the Expressives.

Some congregations think that their pastor must be "a man for all seasons" and a man of all social styles. They demand that their minister constantly display all the positive traits of all four social styles. Such an unrealistic demand will suffocate him. Like everyone else in the congregation, your pastor is only one person with one dominant social style—complete with strengths and weaknesses. Help him reach his potential as a unique individual and he will help you reach yours.

For an excellent presentation of the pastor and his preaching style, read Dr. Tim LaHaye's book, *Your Temperament: Discover Its Potential* (Harvest House Publishers).

4. How does the social styles concept relate to the fruit of the Spirit?

We read in Galatians 5:22-25: "But the fruit of the Spirit is love, joy, peace, patience, kindness, goodness, faithfulness, gentleness, self-control; against such things there is no law. Now those who belong to Christ Jesus have crucified the flesh with its passions and desires. If we live by the Spirit, let us also walk by the Spirit."

The quality or spiritual fruit most needed by all four social styles is love: to love God with all our hearts and to love our neighbors as ourselves. With regard to the remaining fruits in Galatians 5:22-23, all social styles need to display all eight qualities, of course. But by nature, certain social styles struggle more with the expression of some qualities than with others:

- Analyticals usually need to work on expressing joy and faith;
- Drivers usually need to work on expressing patience and gentleness;
- Amiables usually need to work on expressing endurance and peace;
- Expressives usually need to work on expressing self-control and faithfulness.

Raising Children with Style

In general, a basic understanding of the social styles concept can be successfully translated and implemented in child-raising. However, I want to alert you to the biggest conflict area of social styles in child-raising: the crisscross relationship between a parent and a child. As with the crisscross marriage relationship described in chapter 9, the crisscross parent-child relationship will suffer from conflicts in both pace and priorities.

For example, imagine an Analytical parent with an Expressive child. The detail and perfectionism of the parent would be oppressive to the happy-go-lucky child. And the child's let-it-all-hang-out approach to keeping his room would drive the everything-in-its-place parent crazy.

If the parent was an Expressive and the child was an Analytical, there would still be problems. The Expressive parent might have a messy home, cheerfully welcoming anyone at anytime, focusing on making guests feel comfortable. But the Analytical child would probably be too embarrassed to bring his friends home to such a place of disorder.

Potential for conflict also exists with a Driver parent and an Amiable child. The child will try desperately to please his hard-driving, demanding parent, and never quite succeed. Drivers are not known for expressing much appreciation. They believe that a job well done is its own reward. Why reward with compliments something which had to be done?

If the parent is an Amiable and the child is a Driver, the child may run over his parent and lose respect for him because the parent won't stand up to the child.

Social Styles in Education

Here's a little food for thought for those of you involved in education. Research indicates that, in the California school system, 82 percent of all teachers are either Analyticals or Amiables.[1] If this data reflects anything of our country's educational system at large, we may have a large number of Driver and Expressive students whose social style needs are not being understood or met by their teachers. This may especially be true of crisscross teacher-student relationships (Analytical vs. Expressive and Amiable vs. Driver) where pace and priorities conflicts are most prevalent. If you teach others, I recommend that you become alert to the social style needs of all your students, not just those whose styles which are compatible with yours.

Social Styles in the Workplace

If you have the opportunity to select your own staff, or if you have input to the hiring of staff in your workplace, recommend a balance of social styles. If new employees are hired because they have the same style as the boss, I believe that company will encounter large problems. The most effective companies will be those with a rich blend of social styles among the employees.

Your success on the job is related more to your ability to get along with people than to your personal skills. Learn to develop versatility, flexibility and adaptability in relating to the other social styles in your place of employment. Your ability to love God first and love your neighbor second is your greatest asset for advancement and promotion.

If you are in a leadership position, try your best to assign work projects according to social style skills. As much as possible, you want Analyticals and Drivers working on data and products, and Amiables and Expressives working with customers. Your company will serve its patrons well when each staff member is working in his area of strength.

Many people choose their jobs for the monetary reward instead of a fit with their social styles. That's why there are so many unhappy people in the work force. When seeking employment, look for positions which utilize the strengths of your social style. If you are locked into a job which you cannot leave for some reason, try to develop your social style strengths through outside interests. Find your fulfillment in hobbies, sports, clubs, organizations or volunteer work.

Recharging Your Social Style Battery

Nothing drains a task-oriented person as much as dealing with people. When the task-oriented individual feels run down and low on emotional fuel, he can be refilled and recharged through solitude, quietness and task accomplishment. Task-oriented people need times of quiet in order to replenish their capacity for their relationships.

Similarly, relationship-oriented people wear down while performing tasks, especially where social interaction is limited or absent. When a relationship-oriented person runs emotionally low, he needs to pull into the filling station of social interaction and involvement for refueling. A relationship-oriented person must spend quality time with people in order to remain effective in his tasks.

Each of us must be alert to keep our social style batteries charged. Those of us who supervise others must be alert to their needs and make sure they get the solitude or interaction which will keep them happy and productive.

Your positive, loving social style behaviors can be a benefit and blessing in your home, workplace and church. Or your negative, selfish social style behaviors can be the source of disharmony, disunity and disaster wherever you go. May God help us all to be alert and sensitive to His leading in every area of our lives as we learn to get along with people.

Locating Your Own Social Style

To help you locate your social style, turn to pages 33-34 and review your clues for identifying Askers and Tellers. Check the appropriate box under (1) below to record what you discovered about yourself.

Next, turn to pages 39 and 41 and review your clues for identifying Task and Relationship orientation. Check under (2) below how you saw yourself.

Now turn to page 89 and review Back-Against-the-Wall behavior. In the boxes below (3) check the reaction that you most often display (especially at home).

Finally, turn to page 71 and see if you can fine-tune your indication of social style by determining your primary and secondary styles. After reviewing the above, circle the two social style traits in the diagram on the next page that best describe your life-style.

(1) I see myself as more of an:

      □ Asker

      □ Teller

(2) I see myself as more:

      □ Task oriented

      □ Relationship oriented

(3) My Back-Against-the-Wall behavior is more:

      □ To withdraw

      □ To become dogmatic

      □ To give in

      □ To attack

Task Oriented

ANALYTICAL		DRIVER	
Analytical ANALYTICAL	Driver ANALYTICAL	Analytical DRIVER	Driver DRIVER
Amiable ANALYTICAL	Expressive ANALYTICAL	Amiable DRIVER	Expressive DRIVER
Analytical AMIABLE	Driver AMIABLE	Analytical EXPRESSIVE	Driver EXPRESSIVE
Amiable AMIABLE	Expressive AMIABLE	Amiable EXPRESSIVE	Expressive EXPRESSIVE

A S K E R (left side)

T E L L E R (right side)

AMIABLE   **EXPRESSIVE**

Relationship Oriented

Locating Your Family

On the style grid map below, place your name in the appropriate box. Next, place the first names of your family members in their area of social style strength.

This mapping will help you to become aware of your family's social styles, their Back-Against-the-Wall tendencies, areas of possible conflict and your need to adjust your behavior to better reach out to them in love.

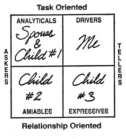

Task Oriented

ANALYTICALS	DRIVERS
Spouse & Child #1	*Me*
Child #2	*Child #3*
AMIABLES	EXPRESSIVES

Relationship Oriented

Example

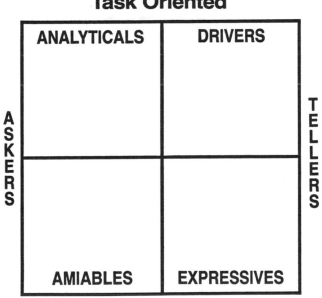

Task Oriented

ANALYTICALS	DRIVERS
AMIABLES	EXPRESSIVES

A S K E R S

T E L L E R S

Relationship Oriented

Locating Your Friends

On the style grid map below, place your name in the appropriate box. Next, place the first names of your friends in their area of social style strength.

This mapping will help you to become aware of your friends' social styles, their Back-Against-the-Wall tendencies, areas of possible conflict and your need to adjust your behavior to better reach out to them in love.

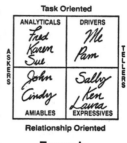

Task Oriented

ANALYTICALS	DRIVERS
Fred Karen Sue	Me Pam
John Cindy	Sally Ken Laura
AMIABLES	EXPRESSIVES

A S K E R S   T E L L E R S

Relationship Oriented

Example

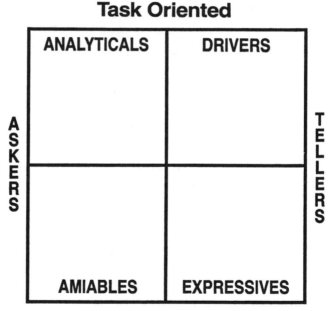

Task Oriented

ANALYTICALS	DRIVERS
AMIABLES	EXPRESSIVES

A S K E R S   T E L L E R S

Relationship Oriented

Locating Fellow Workers

On the style grid map below, place your name in the appropriate box. Next, place the first names of your fellow workers in their area of social style strength.

This mapping will help you to become aware of your fellow workers' social styles, their Back-Against-the-Wall tendencies, areas of possible conflict and your need to adjust your behavior to better reach out to them in love.

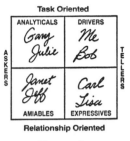

Task Oriented

ANALYTICALS	DRIVERS
Gary	Me
Julie	Bob
Janet	Carl
Jeff	Lisa
AMIABLES	EXPRESSIVES

ASKERS

TELLERS

Relationship Oriented

Example

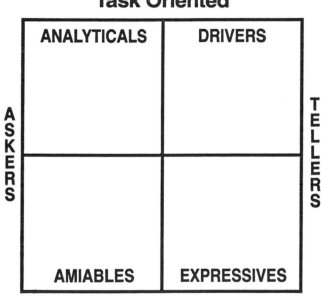

Task Oriented

ANALYTICALS	DRIVERS
AMIABLES	EXPRESSIVES

ASKERS

TELLERS

Relationship Oriented

Notes

Chapter 1
1. Tim LaHaye and Bob Phillips, *Anger Is a Choice* (Grand Rapids, MI: Zondervan Publishing Co., 1982), adapted from p. 23.
2. LaHaye and Phillips, *Anger Is a Choice*, adapted from p. 24.
3. David W. Merrill and Roger H. Reid, *Personal Styles and Effective Performance* (Radnor, PA: Chilton Book Co., 1981), adapted from p. 34.
4. Merrill and Reid, *Personal Styles and Effective Performance*, p. 34.

Chapter 2
1. Merrill and Reid, *Personal Styles and Effective Performance*; Robert Bolton and Dorothy G. Bolton, *Social Style/Management Style* (New York, NY: AMACOM, 1984), adapted.
2. Merrill and Reid, *Personal Styles and Effective Performance*; Bolton and Bolton, *Social Style/Management Style*, adapted.

Chapter 3
1. From the book *Personality Plus* by Florence Littauer, copyright 1983 by Fleming H. Revell Company. Adapted from pp. 22-25. Used by permission of Fleming H. Revell Company.
2. Merrill and Reid, *Personal Styles and Effective Performance*; Bolton and Bolton, *Social Style/Management Style*, adapted.
3. Merrill and Reid, *Personal Styles and Effective Performance*; Bolton and Bolton, *Social Style/Management Style*, adapted.

Chapter 4
1. James C. Hefley, *A Dictionary of Illustrations* (Grand Rapids, MI: Zondervan Publishing Co., 1971), p. 126.
2. Tim LaHaye and Bob Phillips, *Anger Is a Choice* (Grand Rapids, MI: Zondervan Publishing Co., 1982), adapted from p. 23.
3. Anthony J. Alessandra, *Non-Manipulative Selling* (Reston, VA: Reston Publishing Co., 1981), adapted from p. 24.

Chapter 5
1. From the book *Personality Plus* by Florence Littauer, copyright 1983 by Fleming H. Revell Company. Adapted from pp. 85-88. Used by permission of Fleming H. Revell Company.
2. Bolton and Bolton, *Social Style/Management Style*, adapted from p. 48.

Chapter 7
1. Alessandra, *Non-Manipulative Selling*, adapted from p. 28.
2. "Reproduced by special permission of the Publisher, Consulting Psychologists Press, Inc., Palo Alto, CA 94306, from *Gifts Differing* by Isabel Briggs Meyers with Peter B. Myers © 1980. Adapted from pp. 56, 63, 68, 75, 79, 121, 163-164. Further reproduction is prohibited without the Publisher's consent."

Chapter 8
1. Bolton and Bolton, *Social Style/Management Style*, adapted from p. 112.

Chapter 9
1. Author unknown.

Chapter 10
1. Laurence J. Peter, *Peter's Quotations* (New York, NY: Bantam Books, 1979), p. 297.
2. Lloyd Cory, *Quotable Quotes* (Wheaton, IL: Victor Books, 1985), p. 211.
3. E.C. McKenzie, *Mac's Giant Book of Quips and Quotes* (Eugene, OR: Harvest House Publishers, 1980), p. 298.
4. Cory, *Quotable Quotes*, p. 210.
5. Cory, *Quotable Quotes*, p. 211

Chapter 11
1. David Keirsey and Marilyn Bates, *Please Understand Me* (Del Mar, CA: Prometheus Nemesis Book Co. Inc., 1984), p. 155.

Bibliography

Alessandra, Anthony J. *Non-Manipulative Selling.* Reston, VA: Reston Publishing Co., 1981.

Bolton, Robert; and Bolton, Dorothy G. *Social Style/Management Style.* New York, NY: AMACOM, 1984.

Carson, Robert. *Interaction Concepts of Personality.* Chicago, IL: Aldine Publishing Co., 1969.

Cory, Lloyd. *Quotable Quotations.* Wheaton, IL: Victor Books, 1985.

Hallesby, Ole. *Temperament and the Christian Faith.* 1940.

Hefley, James. *A Dictionary of Illustrations.* Grand Rapids: Zondervan Publishing Co., 1971.

Hersey, Paul; and Blanchard, Kenneth H. *Management of Organization Behavior.* Englewood Cliffs, NJ: Prentice-Hall, Inc., 1969.

Keirsey, David; and Bates, Marilyn. *Please Understand Me.* Del Mar, CA: Prometheus Nemesis Book Co. Inc., 1984.

LaHaye, Beverly. *How to Develop Your Child's Temperament.* Eugene, OR: Harvest House Publishers, 1977.

LaHaye, Tim. *Spirit-Controlled Temperament.* Wheaton, IL: Tyndale House Publishers, 1970.

———.*Transformed Temperaments.* Wheaton, IL: Tyndale House Publishers, 1971.

———.*Understanding the Male Temperament.* Old Tappan, NJ: Fleming H. Revell, Co., 1977.

———. *Your Temperament: Discover Its Potential.* Wheaton, IL: Tyndale House Publishers, 1984.

———; and Phillips, Bob. *Anger Is a Choice.* Grand Rapids, MI: Zondervan Publishing Co., 1982.

Leman, Kevin. *The Birth Order Book.* Old Tappan, NJ: Fleming H. Revell, Co., 1985.

Littauer, Florence. *Personality Plus.* Old Tappan, NJ: Fleming H. Revell, Co., 1983.

Mehrabian, Albert. *Silent Messages.* Belmont, CA: Wadsworth Publishing Co., 1971.

Merrill, David W.; and Reid, Roger H. *Personal Styles and Effective Performance.* Radnor, PA: Chilton Book Co., 1981.

Myers, Isabel B.; and Myers, Peter B. *Gifts Differing.* Palo Alto, CA: Consulting Psychologists Press, Inc., 1980.

Peter, Laurence. *Peter's Quotations. New York: Bantam Books, 1977.*

Selye, Hans. Stress without Distress. New York, NY: Harper and Row Publishers, Inc., 1974.

A Leader's Guide for discussion groups using this book, as well as any of the titles below, is available from the author. For a flyer with full descriptions and prices, send a self-addressed, stamped envelope to:

Family Services
P.O. Box 9363
Fresno, CA 93792

OTHER BOOKS BY BOB PHILLIPS

- The World's Greatest Collection of Clean Jokes
- More Good Clean Jokes
- The Last of the Good Clean Joke Books
- The All American Joke Book
- Wit and Wisdom
- The World's Greatest Collection of Heavenly Humor
- In Search of Bible Trivia, Vol. I
- In Search of Bible Trivia, Vol. II
- Redi-Reference
- How Can I Be Sure? A Premarital Inventory
- Praise Is a Three Lettered Word—Joy
- Anger Is a Choice
- The Return of the Good Clean Jokes
- Humor Is Tremendous
- Bible Fun
- God's Hand Over Hume